on toward others, more gentleness with
ae poor, and greater respect for nature."
ike the Jesus of two millennia ago whom
ae Francis of eight centuries ago imitated,
his book proclaims the perennial revolution
f Christianity to today's world.

EONARDO BOFF, O.F.M., has written several
aajor works of liberation theology, most no-
ably *Jesus Christ Liberator*. He received his
octorate from the University of Münster
nd teaches in the major seminary of Petrop-
lis in Brazil.

Saint Francis

SAINT FRANCIS

A MODEL FOR
HUMAN LIBERATION

Leonardo Boff

Translated by John W. Diercksmeier

CROSSROAD · NEW YORK

1982

The Crossroad Publishing Company
575 Lexington Avenue, New York, N.Y. 10022

Originally published under the title *São Francisco de Assis:
Ternura e Vigor* by Vozes/Cefepal, Petropolis, Brazil, 1981
English translation copyright © 1982 by
The Crossroad Publishing Company

Printed in the United States of America

Library of Congress Cataloging in Publication Data

Boff, Leonardo.
  Saint Francis: a model for human liberation.

  Translation of: São Francisco de Assis.
  1. Francis, of Assisi, Saint, 1182–1226. 2. Church
and the poor. 3. Liberation theology. I. Title.
BX4700.F6B5613 1982   271'.3'024   82-14152
ISBN 0-8245-0488-7

*To my brother friars Luis Flavio Cappio
and Enrique Salvador de Mello, who opted to live
with the poor and like the poor, according to
the grand inheritance of the "Fratello" and
"Poverello" Francis of Assisi.*

Contents

Introduction

Whenever the saints, in their following of Christ, plumb the depths of human existence, there appears the perennial truth of the Gospel. They break the boundaries of their times and become contemporaries of every time and every person in search of their star. And because of this, they are neither ancient nor modern; they are simply true, always true, carriers of that truth that captures the crucial questions of existence in every age, as well as the very truth of Christ.

The five questions presented here are like concentric circles, from the most general to the most particular. The first one deals with the problem of the *system* in which we live: the crisis of the forms of consumerism and of the rational. Francis brings out in us other principles of structure, those deep within the heart—tenderness and communion with nature. The second question is that of contemporary *society;* it represents a fissure from top to bottom: the division between rich and poor, overabundance on the one hand and need on the other, leading to injustices on worldwide levels. Francis, the Little Poor Man, lived a radical expropriation as a form of solidarity with the poor and with the poor Christ. The meaning of human life is not found in creating riches but fraternity; it is supported not by having but by being one with and compassionate with all creatures. The third question is that of *integral liberation.* The entire system and the whole of society is marked by uncontainable desires for liberation, on the part of the oppressed and the poor. Francis emerges as one of the most liberated saints of the Christian experience, with that freedom that comes from the Gospel of Jesus Christ Liberator. Francis, also called the Brother, liberates through goodness, with the trust that he places in the secret energies of light, which are ignited in every heart and which no sin or oppression can extinguish.

The fourth question is that of *ecclesiogenesis,* that is to say, the ongoing genesis of the Church. The Church is not only an ancient institution linked to its founders—Christ, the Holy Spirit, the apostles, and the prophets—but it is primarily a faith event, born as a response to the Word, *sponsa Verbi,* heard and lived in the wide arena of the world, not only in the closed walls of churches and monasteries. Francis created a popular expression of the Church; the mystery of the Church becomes concrete in the small fraternities of brothers in contact with the people and with the poorest of the people of God.

The fifth question has to do with the problem of the *integration of the negative in life.* The human path is structured like a great theatrical drama: every ascent takes place as a liberation from multiple supports, all sanctity is built upon the backdrop of great temptations, and as long as we live, sin always costars with grace. Francis opened a new path in the conquering of his own heart; he made of the very dimension of shadows a path to God with his great simplicity and humility. Because of this, he sings as much about life and love as he does about illness and death; they are integrated as brothers and sisters in the great family of God.

These five questions are treated from the perspective of the poor, because they are the ones who are most interested in qualitative changes in our world. The vision of the poor helps more than any other to identify the red-hot issues and to find the liberating solutions for the vast majority of them. Furthermore, Francis of Assisi made himself the Little Poor Man among the poor, and from them tried to read the Gospel and all of reality.

Finally, we humbly apply to ourselves the words of this Seraphic Father: "It is a great shame, for us servants of God, that the saints do the work and we, talking about them, want to receive the same glory and honor" (*Admonitions* 6).

Assisi, Rome, Petropolis
October 1981

Saint Francis

A MODEL OF GENTLENESS AND CARE

On one occasion, Brother Bonaventure, the gardener of the friary at the Portiuncula, climbing Mount Subasio with a brother from a faraway country, was asked what Franciscan spirituality is. Brother Bonaventure, a simple and very spiritual man, in a sweet voice made more so by his Umbrian accent, responded: "Franciscan spirituality is Saint Francis. And who is Saint Francis? It is enough to utter his name and everyone knows who he is. Saint Francis was a man of God. And because he was a man of God, he always lived what is essential. And so he was simple, courteous, and gentle with everyone, like God in His mercy."

The little old Fiat bounces along the rocky road that leads to the friary at the Carceri. There below, spread out and lit by the pleasant autumn sun, is the peaceful valley of Assisi, like a woven tapestry of houses and farms. Suddenly Brother Bonaventure stops the car and jumps out; but it is not to contemplate the wide panorama before him, from the heights above the cliffs to the valley below. Rather, with his Franciscan eyesight, he has discovered little white flowers among the abundant greenery. "Look at how beautiful they are!" says the brother, rough but with a refined spirit, as he leans over them, like someone leaning over the crib of a newborn child.

The brother from the faraway country discovers some mulberries, green and ripe, and he tastes them. "Why do you take the green mulberries, Brother?" interrupts Brother Bonaventure. "Don't you see that they suffer? Would you cut someone down in the prime of life? Only when they are older do they offer themselves gladly for our enjoyment."

The descent is as slow as the climb. The small car descends the mountain smoothly. "Why don't we go a bit faster, Brother Bonaventure?" He answers: "There is no reason to abuse the good nature of the car. For eighteen years it has carried me to and fro, and it has always been good to me. Should I not show it some consideration by avoiding rough braking with so many curves?"

Then, back at the Portiuncula, he shows me his garden, full of vegetables, grape vines, fig trees, and many flowers. I also see a disorderly bush, bright green in color. "Brother Bonaventure, what is that?" He says, with an innocent smile: "They are our sisters, the weeds. I let them grow there because they too are daughters of God and they sing of the beauty of God."

It is Sunday, and there is a celebration in the friary because the new superior of the house begins his term of office. A special wine is served. Brother Bonaventure drinks his wine in silence and with deep respect. He does so as if he were taking part in a ritual of some sort. "What is it, Brother?" And he, in almost a whisper, says: "I must honor Brother Wine. I myself made it, six years ago. And it too is joyful in our joy."

Brother Francis still lives in his "little poor ones." All of his penances and foolishness were worth the trouble in order to liberate and allow the birth of a spirit as gentle and brotherly as that of Brother Bonaventure. Francis lives and is among us, hidden within each one of us. I saw him born again in the attitudes of Brother Bonaventure.

I, brother from a faraway country, minor theologian, outcast and sinner—I saw him and I give witness. In praise of Christ. Amen.

========

The crisis that we are all suffering is structural in nature and concerns the basics of our system of life together.[1] This is the reason for its dramatic and undeniable character. The crisis of the global system derives from the crisis specific to the ruling class, the bourgeois class that has directed our history for the past five centuries. The ethos of this class, that is, its practices and the meaning that is given to them, the forms of relationships that consecrated and gave rise to the rest of the social classes, shows itself more or less incapable of assimilating, within its own structure, new and emerging forms, just as it is incapable of developing from its own resources an alternative that is meaningful for everyone. We find ourselves at the end of one era and at the beginning of a new one. Within this context, the figure of Francis is a highly appealing one.

THE END OF THE ECONOMY OF THE LOGOS

The phenomenological manifestations of this crisis present an awesome specter: emptiness, loneliness, fear, anxiety, aggressiveness without objectives, in a word, general dissatisfaction. Emptiness is born of a feeling of impotence, that there is little we can do to change our own life and that of society, and finally, that nothing is important. Loneliness is expressive of the loss of contact with nature and others in terms of friendship and gentleness; there is the lack of courage to commit ourselves. Fear is the fruit of the objective threats to life, to employment, to the collective survival of humanity in general. Anxiety has its origin in imagined fear, ignorance as to what one ought to do, in whom to trust, and what to expect; when anxiety grips an entire society, it means that the whole society feels threatened and senses its approaching end. Generalized aggressiveness reveals a rupture with the norms of relationship without which a society cannot be built or defended; what results is anonymity and the loss of the meaning of the Self, that is, the worth and sacredness of the human person. From all of this there derives two consequences no less serious: emptiness and the loss of the language of everyday communication, the loss of meaningful personal relationships and the loss of the vital relationship with nature. And to any empty, threatened, anxious, and aggressive individual this same nature appears mute, indifferent, and dead. A similar absence of enthusiasm aids the breakdown of the ecosystems. This adds to, generally, the excesses of irrationality, which reveal the limitations of the system of social integration. The old myths are in agony and the new ones do not yet have sufficient strength to give birth to a new cultural ethos.

This crisis constitutes, as we have said, the crisis of the dominant class. The classes below are not immune to it, but they have other reasons for living and struggling. As we will see, they are the bearers of alternative solutions, capable of teaching and forming a new society.

These few phenomenological facts are symptoms, not causes. The ontological root of this crisis ought to be sought much deeper within reality and much farther back in time.[2] It is linked to the appearance of the bourgeoisie as a social class, from the heart of the feudal system itself. The development of the world of the artisans creating the market system gave rise to a new meaning for being: the desire for wealth, for goods, for power. Together with this a new ethos was developed, that is, a new way of life with different relationships to nature, to others, to religion, and to God. Science and technology did not arise as pure and free responses to reason but rather as answers demanded by the rise of production, of the marketplace, and of consumerism. They constitute the decisive contribution of the bourgeoisie to humanity. Because of production, the rationality that was developed to its utmost was analytic-instrumental reason, to the detriment of other forms of reason (dialectic, wisdom, etc.). Knowing has its own defined irrationality: power. Power and knowing go hand in hand for the modern upper class. Because of this, the scientific and technological projects would become the big business of the dominant system of the world as part of the process of production.[3]

The individual of the modern upper class is above things and no longer with them, because analytical knowledge means the power of control over the mechanisms designed for human enjoyment. Analytic rationality demands a cutting off of the other legitimate avenues to the real, those described as Pathos, sympathy, or Eros, fraternal communication and tenderness. This whole dimension will be marked and even denounced as disturbing to scientific objectivity. Science at the service of the a priori founders (desire for wealth, for realization) organizes its demarche of domination through the projection of models and paradigms of reality that guarantees its operative efficiency. Certainly this pragmatism has its reason for being (to guarantee the production and reproduction of life); but, nevertheless, it is profoundly diminishing in that it categorizes and artificializes reality, and hides the meaningful dimensions for the realization of the human meaning of life. In spite of the enthusiasm surrounding the discoveries at the beginning of the modern revolution, nature was separated from the emotional and archetypal life of people; it stopped being one of the great sources of the symbolic and sacramental dimensions of life, losing its therapeutic and humanizing functions.

Obviously, human beings did not cease to feel, to live, and to relate in other ways. But all of this took place under the rule of reason, installed as the supreme judge before whom all things must render accounts. There were long periods wherein it was thought that science and technology was the only integrating principle of every culture, the redemption for the secular wounds of humanity. The belief in this myth gave way to one sole picture of all known peoples, at great cultural cost.

Today we live beneath this demand: almost everything is organized in view of productivity. Production is geared toward the consumer market. Consumerism is geared toward satisfying real needs, especially those artificially induced by advertising. The upper class, primary bearer of the modern historical project, realized for itself the ideals of its founding fathers: to create a society of plenty. But it did so at an exorbitant social cost, giving rise to inequalities and levels of exploitation and insufferable poverty, according to humanistic and ethical criteria. The marginated sectors of society do not suffer a crisis of meaning, but rather, on the contrary, find meaning in the struggle for life and in the commitment to the historical improvement of the modern bourgeois system. The dominant system is being corroded from within, without hope and without a future. What does one do after having won the battle of hunger, having satisfied one's needs to the point of nausea? Having reduced the meaning of existence to the satisfying of these needs, once they are met one does not know what else to do. The dominant upper class has accomplished its historical mission, and it must be replaced by some other historical subject, operator of some other hope and agent of some other social meaning.

The ultimate roots of the present impasse of rationality go even farther back: they are found at the dawn of our culture, in the great turn from the pre-Socratics to the Socratics, when the Logos took its own path, overtaking the Mythos, and the concept gained dominion over the symbol. With Aristotle we already practically have the system of reason, with its drive to order, classify, systematize, and dominate. But the historical consequences of the system of reason were only manifested with the emergence of the upper class in the sixteenth century. This class transformed reason into a great system of domination of the world, as well as of social revolution (the French Revolution). Everything points to the fact that we are arriving at the end of this long process, not at the end of reason—that would be absurd—but at the end of its total rule.[4]

The modern postwar critic, conscious of the apocalyptic danger that reason, turned in on itself, can produce, points out the limitations of the whole historical project of science and technology. In the first place, there exists an internal limitation: growth cannot be unlimited, because the universe is finite and nonrenewable energy is reduced. Second, the absolute reign of reason tore to pieces the surrounding world and deeply distorted all social relationships. Reason became more and more antagonistic toward those dimensions of life that were less productive, though more receptive. The Logos accented Eros and Pathos, the values of direct contact, of intimacy and affectivity, of creativity and fantasy, of simplicity and spontaneity. Eros and Techne seem to live in constant battle. "The lover, like the poet, is a threat to assembly-line production. Eros breaks existing molds and creates new molds; and that, naturally, is a threat to technology, which demands regularity, foresight, and is controlled by the clock. Untamed Eros fights against all concepts and limits of time."[5] The spirit of geometry needs to come to agreement with the spirit of refinement (Pascal); logic needs to live alongside courtesy, because both are expressions of the human.

THE BEGINNING OF THE REIGN OF EROS AND PATHOS

Everywhere the need is felt to broaden the use of rationality far beyond instrumental-technocratic rationality. This need not be hegemonic, but is indispensable to insure the material basis for the other forms in which the reciprocity of the consciousness, liberty, creativity, sympathy, and tenderness may be articulated. There must be found channels of power that border upon innocence in its literal sense, that is, that do not harm the relationship with others and with nature.[6] In this sense, at the beginning of a new cultural dawning, we may dream of the beginning of a new reign, that of Eros and Pathos.[7] On this plane, the figure of Saint Francis shines forth as a reference point and basis for hope. However, before we analyze the cultural significance of the man from Assisi, we must have a greater theoretical clarity about the meaning of this emerging rule of Eros and Pathos.

Before all else, it is necessary to point out some preconcepts that cause interminable difficulties. Some contrast the rationalism of the modern era and irrationality, as if it were human to live without the integration of the regulating function of reason. Irrationality as lived in the twentieth century, with the tragedies that it caused through racism, nationalism, and other totalitarian ideologies, is as noxious, if not more so, than rationalism itself. Others contrast love and power, linking them in an inverse relationship: the more the power, the less the love, and vice versa. This opposition also takes place on a superficial and psychological level. Love is understood as a subjective emotion and power as compulsion and domination. On an ontological level, power is power to be, a condition for love itself. Love, ontologically, is the power of giving, of surrender, or the capacity to accept the other as other. Love and power are not mutually reducible, but maintain dialectical relationships between each other: "Love needs power in order to be something more than sentimentalism, just as power needs love in order not to end by being manipulated."[8] The one must be articulated with the other in order to accurately describe reality.

Second, it is necessary to decide what the ultimate base of human existence is. We have already said that the Greek Logos is at the root of our culture, and the Cartesian *cogito* at the origin of modernity. With the evolution of reflection, we came to discover that reason does not explain or touch upon everything. There exists the arational and the irrational; it appears that the tragedy lies more in history than in reason itself. Reason, as expressed by the philosopher Jean Ladriere, is not the first or the last moment of human existence.[9] It is open to what is below and to what is above. From below there emerges something older, deeper, more elementary and primitive—affectivity. From above, reason is open to the spiritual experience that is the discovery of the totality present in the ego, not as pure contemplation, but rather as an experience that beyond the concrete there are not only structures but gratifying feeling, sympathy, and tenderness.

The base experience is feeling. Not the *cogito, ergo sum* (I think, therefore I am), but the *sentio, ergo sum* (I feel, therefore I am); not

Logos, but Pathos, the capacity to be affected and to affect—affectivity. This is the concrete and primary *Lebenswelt* of human beings. Existence is never pure existence; it is an existence felt and affected by joy or sadness, by hope or anguish, strength, repentance, goodness.

The primary relationship is a relationship without distance, of profound active passivity, in the sense of feeling the I, the world, others. It is a being with, not above; it is a coliving, communing in the same reality not yet differentiated; as Heidegger would say, the revelation of existence in its fundamental and constitutive ties, like the world in its totality.[10] The ontological basis for depth psychology (Freud, Jung, Adler, and their disciples) lies in this conviction: the ultimate structure of life is feeling, not only as a movement of the psyche, but as an "existential quality," the ontic structuring of the human being. Such a being is affectivity, as a mode of being, and not only the human psyche.

It is important to underscore that Pathos (feeling) is not in opposition to Logos (rational comprehension). Feeling is also a form of knowledge, but more comprehensive and enveloping than reason. It embraces reason within itself, releasing it in all directions. The genius who saw this was Pascal, one of the founders of the science of probability, the builder of the calculator, affirming that the primary axioms of thought are intuited by the heart and that it is the heart that determines the premises for all possible knowledge of the real.[11] Knowledge by way of Pathos (feeling) is achieved by sym-pathy, by feeling together with perceived reality, and by em-pathy, or identification with perceived reality.

Ancient man, before the hegemony of reason, lived a mystic union with all realities, including God; he felt umbilically linked with the surrounding world and with his own intimacy; he participated in the nature of all things and they participated in his nature. This took place because the feeling of belonging and of universal familiarity allowed a harmonious integration of human existence with respect and veneration of all the elements. And this was so because he lived the truly archaic structure of life, that is, in the heart of the principle and the origin of knowledge (the etymological meaning of *archaic:* from *arche*, principle, origin). The postmodern individual is in search of the lost accord that survives, especially, in dreams, in regressive and progressive utopias, and in fertile imagination. But this is not enough; one must realize it in a historical project, not through the mere redressing of the old, but by means of a new embracing synthesis of the tradition of the Logos to which we belong. But first we must outline in more detail the structure of the Pathos.

The "Demonic" Strength of Eros

Pathos is not only affectivity, that is, to feel affected by existence itself and by the world in its totality; it is primarily becoming active and taking the initiative of feeling and identifying with perceived reality. To live is to feel, and to feel is to capture the value of things; value is the precious character of things, that which makes them worthy of being and that which makes them appealing. Eros, in the classic sense we give it here, is that force that with enthusiasm, joy, and passion makes us search for union with the things we perceive and appreciate, with our own realization, with the significant persons in our world, with our ideals, with our vocation, with God. An archaic myth from ancient Greece describes it better than any definition: "Eros, the god of love, arose to create the world. Before, everything had been silence, naked and immobile. Now, everything is life, joy, movement." This is the real essence of Eros: life that searches passionately for life, the joy of existence, the movement that enlivens, widens, deepens, and transforms. The basic dynamic of reality, also human, is constituted by Eros. In the beginning there was not reason but passion (Pathos and Eros). The proper impulse of reason to know, order, and dominate comes through Eros, which resides in it. It is responsible for the mysticism that consumes the scientist in search of the keys to the structure of the real. Eros does not only imply a feeling, but a co-feeling, a consent; not only being conscious of the passion of the world, but having com-passion; it is not a living, but a living together, a sympathizing and an entering into communion. What is proper to Eros is to unite subject with object; but to unite with compassion, with enthusiasm, with desire. There is fire and heat in Eros. Everything that is tied to Eros must see with fantasy, with creativity, bursting forth toward the new, the surprising, the wonderful. Eros produces fascination, attraction, and enchantment. The ancients said that it is a *daimon:* what is hidden within it is a "demonic" force, the vulcanicity of the elements in ferment. The best way of representing the human spirit for us is to consider it as Eros,[12] because the life of the spirit is never represented as something ready-made and finished, but rather as a process and project of execution, deepening, retreating and recovering, searching out new molds, and rising above and beyond every determination.

Sex and Eros (whose identification brought so many errors into our culture) are related, but are not the same thing. The great ontologically based psychoanalyst Rollo May affirms rightly: "Sex is a rhythm of stimulus and response, Eros is a state of being. The goal of sex is the gratification and relief of tension, while that of Eros is desire, hope and the eternal search for expansion." The supreme expression of Eros is oblative love, which, through communion with the other, surrenders itself in disinterested joy and in service to the loved one or to God. Through the strength of Eros, love maintains its fidelity; the missionary reaffirms his or her commitment to the most backward people in a wild jungle or in the middle of the physical misery of a run-down ghetto. There runs through Eros a permanent push toward the higher, the more beautiful, the more true, the more just, and the more human. Not without reason, the Platonic-Augustinian tradition saw in Eros the push that leads us to God and toward the mystic flight of union with him, and finally, toward ecstasy.[14]

Humanized Eros: Gentleness and Care

Because of its irruptive character, Eros always runs the risk of being perverted by *epithymia*, concupiscence. It can degenerate into something orgiastic and other forms of destructive enjoyment. The free rein of impulsiveness without a consciousness of limits, the instinct to celebrate value without discerning what is a just value (all values are valid, but not so for every circumstance), can call forth the depersonalizing demons of existence and culture. It is like a dam that bursts; the dikes break, everything is destruction, and water is spread everywhere until it finds borders that cause it to form a river. Freud clearly saw that a civilization is only built upon the disciplining of Eros.

Within this context, Logos, or reason, enters and plays an irreplaceable role. It is proper to reason to see clearly, to order and discipline. It is proper to reason to confer form and to define the direction of Eros. But it is important to understand the relative character of Logos and Eros. In the beginning is Eros and not Logos. As we have already stated, the latter rises out of the former. And here there arises one of the most difficult and dramatic dialectics in the history of the spirit. Logos, by nature, tends to dominate everything within its path; there exists the risk of subjugating and tripping up Eros, instead of granting it form and discipline. The drama of modern culture lies precisely in its repression of Eros. The ruling of the Logos brought forth repressive ways of life, stunted creativity, and fantasy; it placed under suspicion all pleasure and feeling; the anima, in its spreading of gentleness, conviviality, and compassion, was entombed by the inflation of the animus. We have already said that coldness, the lack of enthusiasm for life, the feeling that nothing is worth the trouble, and the great mechanisms of repression and control are consequences of the exacerbation of the Logos and of the trampling down of the energies of Eros. For the rest, the monopoly of the system and of order, introduced by reason, never stopped being contested throughout history. Today this tendency is almost universal, which presages the blossoming of a new balance, without the tyranny of reason over the spontaneity of Eros, with the possibility of living together unrepressed and unmarked by anxiety. Herbert Marcuse, dissenting from Freud, made it very clear that the original force that creates culture is not so much repressive sublimation as the free development of Eros, which is dependent on the Logos to regulate itself, without at the same time allowing itself to be subjugated by the Logos's dominating dynamic. The struggle for existence is, originally, a struggle for the reign of Eros. Culture begins when collective forms for its expansion are found. In the past, however, the struggle for existence was organized in the interest of security and domination on the part of the Logos, thus transforming the "erotic" foundation of the culture. "When philosophy conceived of the essence of being as Logos, it is already the Logos of imperative domination, dominant, oriented to reason, to which man and nature must be subject."[15]

What happens when Eros is able, at one and the same time, to assure its own rule and yet discipline itself by means of the right use of the Logos? The result is gentleness through the just utilization of the Logos. There arise, then, gentleness and care as the basic elements of a person and of a culture. When Eros remains completely free, as the uncontrolled exuberance of feelings and passions, sentimentalism, the unleashing of the emotions, the delirium of impulses, the orgiastic ecstasy of pleasure is unleashed. When Logos is allowed to impose its dominion, rigidity, and inflexibility, the tyranny of the norm, the domination of order, the rigor of discipline flourish. In the first case, the seed of life is drowned by overwatering; in the second, it dries up for lack of water. In both cases, a dehumanizing of existence is harvested.

When, on the other hand, Eros releases the torrent of its enthusiasm[16] by means of the disciplinary force of the Logos, then there arises the concomitance of two characteristics: gentleness and strength. Gentleness, or also care, is the compassionate Eros, capable of feeling and communing with the other, which is not detained in the enjoyment of its own desires, but rather rests in the other with tenderness and love. Because of this, gentleness and care must pay attention to the other, being attentive to the other's structure, showing solicitude, growing with the other.

Gentleness and care are something very different from sentimentality. Sentimentality is a problem of subjectivity: the subject who is centered in his own feeling, beginning and ending with himself. Gentleness and care, on the contrary, imply the decentralization of the subject from himself and concentration on the object of the relationship. Through gentleness and care the object is perceived in itself; the person senses the other person as other and loves him or her; the person goes out to the other and is fascinated by the other. The object occupies and determines the subject. The subject allows passion and compassion to arise from the object. He lingers in the other, not because of the sensation the other evokes in him, but because of the other as other, because of the fascination that the other causes. In gentleness, fascination is not troubling, because there is neither the struggle for power nor the will for domination or for self-gratification, but rather serenity and strength. There is a brilliance that is not blinding but that fits the circumstance and the person. Gentleness and care are Eros in its balance and rule.

Gentleness is gentleness because it contains strength within itself. Strength is the presence of the Logos within Eros, but at the service of the manifestation of Eros. Strength is contention without domination, law without legalism, defined direction without intolerance, development without enslavement. The Logos is for Eros what the retaining wall is for the immensity of waters behind a dam. Only because of that wall can the waters move the turbines and generate energy, lighting the cities of men.

Gentleness and care create the universe of excellences, existential meanings, all that is of value and importance and because of which it is worth sacrificing one's time, energies, and life itself. The basic root of our cultural crisis resides in the terrifying lack of gentleness and care of each other, of nature, and of our own future.

It is not without reason that a philosopher as wise as Martin Heidegger defines gentleness (*Fürsorge*) and care (*Sorge*) as the structural phenomena of existence,[17] as was already related in the old Greek myth, according to which the god Care brought existence into being.[18]

Blaise Pascal calls gentleness and care *the spirit of kindness* as counterposed to *the spirit of geometry:* "This has a slow, hard, and inflexible way of seeing; the former has a flexibility of thought that is applied at one and the same time to the many parts of that which is loved."[19] The heart (the dimension of the heart) is the organ of the spirit of kindness; it produces cordiality, which is the synonym of gentleness and care. Heart, for Pascal, does not mean the expression of emotion in a psychological sense, as opposed to logic; it is not feeling as opposed to intellect; but, in an ontological sense, it is the capacity of the spirit to capture the axiological character of being, its fascination and brilliance. It is Eros in the ontological language of the Greeks (not totally reducible to the Freudian Eros), and because of this, the primary constitutive element of human existence. The heart and the spirit of kindness constitute the central reality of the human being and of a humanizing culture.

Toward a Civilization of Conviviality

The great postwar search is one for alternatives to the dominant culture produced by science and technology, which put the reality of the Apocalypse within our reach. We cannot continue on this path: it has already given all it can give. Necrophilic dimensions are being manifested today. A new rooting is being sought. This does not mean that we may avoid science and technology. What is in question is not science and technology, but their tyranny, the monopoly that they hold on the organization of human interaction.

We need these tools to organize the collective satisfaction of our basic needs. But the cultural operation of guaranteeing the production and reproduction of life must be housed within some other system of reference, in which science and technology may be liberated from their dominating and hegemonic character.

What are these alternatives? The great debate is found precisely in this search for viable alternatives. It is not enough to review the historical path of Logos that produced science and technology. Philosophical, anthropological, psychoanalytical, and theological reflection have practically exhausted this phase. It is important to move from the anticulture to a development of elements of an alternative culture. This is the urgent question before us: Under the reign of what dimension (value, choice, structure, etc.) are the rest of the elements organized (primarily science and technology) that are unavoidable for the stage of development in which we find ourselves? Is it possible to create a new cultural unit? If it does not seem possible to create anything more than an integration, at least the space is given for a composite unity,[20] whose coherence comes through action. Institutions (such as science, technology, or any other) are maintained, developed, and continually recreate a meaning for being through action. Action is instituting not instituted; in spite of any previous conditioning, the originating creativity of human existence is achieved. Through action, the diverse pieces of a culture, no matter how far apart they may be, enter into contact and interaction. Action is, in itself, the creator of culture.

What type of action is imperative for the postmodern individual? The conscious action of respect, care, gentleness, cordiality, and conviviality. However, this will only be possible if modern man radically questions the meaning of life and being that has been a given for the last few centuries. He will not yet be able, without the most serious risk of self-destruction, to understand the meaning of being as domination and being-over-things. His existence is not summed up only by this manner of speaking. One can also co-live, be open with respect to confraternization, adding dimensions of gentleness and cordiality with all things. But this is only possible if life and culture are organized beneath the rule of Eros, and no longer that of the Logos. This is not only a question of a collective decision to be made, but of a conscious practice and education. It is necessary to let blossom the archaic structures of life that are constituted, as we have already said, by Eros, by feeling, by the ordering of the heart. Ivan Illich used the expression *conviviality.*[21] Through conviviality, a different use is made of the immense scientific and technical tools placed at our disposal, not primarily for accumulation, unchecked and selfish satisfaction, and the activation of the principle of ownership, but rather the primacy of gift, liberty, and incentive to the meaning of being.

Giving more room to Eros—that is, to creative spontaneity, freedom, fantasy, the ability to demonstrate gentleness and care—there will arise a multidimensional balance able to guarantee a more human and integrated form of life, with nature and with others.

The strength of movements that search for a new meaning for living linked to earthly roots, to simplicity, to respect, to gentleness with others and the care of nature will take on a worldwide dimension. A new hegemony will begin: that of Eros and Pathos.

Who is the principal channel for this way of being? The most visible representatives are youth, children of the modern era, offshoots of the Enlightenment, descendants of the masters of suspicion (Nietzsche, Marx, Freud). They do not want to continue to be the agents of the rationalistic system of domination. But there is an entire social class, a new and emerging historical subject, the peoples and worker strata, the decisive channels of the new cultural model. The struggle for life, work, exploitation made the popular masses the guardians of those values we so often miss: hospitality, cordiality, collaboration, solidarity, the sense of respect for the sacredness of God and of natural things, especially life. It does not cease to be symptomatic that one of the greatest revolutionaries of our time, Ché Guevara, adopted this slogan for his actions: "One must be hard, but without losing tenderness." The same gentleness is apparent in many of the attitudes of union leaders,[22] sensitive to small symbolic gestures, yet filled with historical import because they preserve the secret of all transforming power: the mystique, the desire, and the enthusiasm for change.

FRANCIS, POSTMODERN BROTHER: THE TRIUMPH OF COMPASSION AND GENTLENESS

In this context of the crisis of the dominant culture and of the search for alternative paths, the figure of Saint Francis of Assisi shines forth as highly significant and desirable. Every search needs reference points and archetypes that inspire it. A culture needs historical personalities who serve as mirrors in which that culture may see itself and be convinced of the values that give meaning to being. For our age, Francis is more than a saint of the Catholic Church and founder of the Franciscan family. He is the purest figure (gestalt) of Western history, of the dreams, the utopias, and of the way of relating panfraternally that we are all searching for today. He speaks to the most archaic depths of the modern soul, because there is a Francis of Assisi hidden within each one of us, struggling to emerge and expand freely among the moles of the modern age.

What most impresses modern humanity when faced with the figure of Saint Francis of Assisi is his innocence, his enthusiasm for nature, his gentleness with all beings, his capacity for compassion with the poor and of confraternization with all the elements, and even with death itself. Rollo May states: "Innocence is the preservation of an infantile clarity at an adult age. Everything retains its freshness, its purity, its newness and color. It leads to spirituality; it is the innocence of Saint Francis of Assisi in his preaching to the birds."[23] And here is where all of the fascination with Saint Francis is found. Max Scheler called him the Western World's most characteristic representative of the way of relating with empathy and sympathy:

> It deals with a unique encounter between Eros and Agape (an Agape deeply penetrated by *amor Dei* and *amor in Deo*), in an especially holy and genial soul; it deals with an interpretation of both (Eros and Agape) so perfect that it is the greatest and most sublime example of a spirituality of matter, and at the same time, of a materialization of spirit that I have ever been given to know. Never again in the history of the West does there emerge a figure marked with such a strength of sympathy and of universal emotion as that of Saint Francis. No one has better achieved the unity and integrity of all elements than did Saint Francis in the realm of the religious, the erotic, social relations, art, and knowledge. Better yet, the proper characteristic of all previous time is in that the strong unity lived by Saint Francis was diluted in a growing multiplicity of figures, also marked by emotion and heart in the most diverse movements, but articulated in a unilateral way.[24]

Essentially, Francis liberated the springs of the heart and the outpouring of Eros. He is the sun of Assisi, as Dante called him.[25] He achieved an admirable accord between Logos and Pathos, between Logos and Eros. He demonstrated with his life that, to be a saint, it is necessary to be human. And to be human, it is necessary to be sensitive and gentle. With the poor man from Assisi fell the veils that covered reality. When this happens, it remains evident that human reality is not a rigid structure, not a concept, but rather it is sympathy, capacity for compassion and gentleness.[26] Because in this way, one can laugh and cry at almost the same time, and even facing death it is possible to sing *cantilenae amatoriae*. In other words, the sinner Adam and the innocent Job are assumed by him with infinite compassion and tenderness.[27] Sigmund Freud would have recognized that Francis was perhaps someone who carried the expression of love the farthest, who was able to relate to the strangest beings.[28] In effect, in Francis one can see the sovereign rule of Eros over Logos, a communion and confraternalization with all of reality such as has never been seen since. We will outline a little better the basic experience of Saint Francis.

Francis and the Eruption of Eros and Desire

Eros constitutes the basic dynamic and the main force of human existence. As Freud excellently showed, the manifestation of Eros is principally given by way of desire. Desire, for its part, as Aristotle taught,[29] is by nature unlimited (*apeiron*). All actions try to satisfy it, fundamentally, without doing so. Because of this, the human search is revealed as insatiable and full of anxiety, because desire remains ever present and ever new. Francis emerges as one of the most prodigious manifestations of Eros and desire.[30] Through the force of Eros and insatiable desire everything seems new in him; everything is begun anew with the same initial enthusiasm.[31] What has been assumed is achieved through total surrender. The *Legend of the Three Companions* says candidly: "He suffered great perplexity of spirit, and did not rest until he had achieved the dreamed-of ideal; he was racked by diverse thoughts that harshly disturbed him. Divine fire burned, completely, within him."[32] What was the desire that burned in his heart? The first biographers are in agreement about this: "This was his supreme philosophy, this the most vivid desire while he lived: to ask of wise and simple men, perfect and imperfect, small and great alike, how one might best arrive at the height of perfection."[33] And when he discovers in the gospel of commission the will of God for him, he exclaims:

"This is what I most desire, to this do I aspire with all my soul. . . . This is what I want to put into practice with all of my strength."[34] Giving up everything led him to identify with the poor and with the poor Christ, because "above all things he desired to dissolve and unite himself with Christ."[35] The desire to be united with all things led to the mysticism of the cosmic fraternity and in the unity with the All, expressed in the "Canticle of Brother Sun." Finally, on Mount Alverna, his desire for union with the Crucified burst forth in his own body in the form of five wounds.

Only those who desire the impossible achieve what is possible within human limits. Francis was taken by the desire for radicalness. What he understood and what he proposed he lived out to its logical conclusion. There did not exist for him theory on the one hand and practice on the other.[36] Both coexist in him in an impressive manner. And so, his axiom is: "Man knows as much as he does."[37] The vigorous strength of his Eros explains the mysterious coherence that there was between what he said and the constancy with which he lived the radicalness of poverty with passion and gentleness. He incarnated the myth, visibly reproduced the archetype of the perfect imitation of Christ made human. The fascination that he exercised among his generation and over all persons even today is owed to the bursting eruption of his Eros and desire, awakening the Eros of every individual who comes into contact with his figure. Saint Bonaventure says graciously: "The desire that inspired so many activities (preaching the Gospel to the sultan in Morocco) was so powerful that, despite his bodily weakness, he went ahead of his companion on the pilgrimage, and as if drunk with the spirit, flew in haste to reach his goal."[38] This is a reference to the powerful energy of Eros that boiled within him.[39] Without that Eros there is no ascent to God, nor a decided search for human perfection. Francis is the one who overcomes the instinct for compromise and the law of least resistance. He is the one who "endemonizes" existence to try new paths in the direction of an ever greater utopia.

Penance, the Price of Gentleness

With Eros as the basic operator of existence, Francis opened the gates of freedom, drive, and spontaneous expansion of personal experience. Essentially, one can perceive in his entire practice the valuation of his personal Pathos, as well as that of every one of the brothers that the Lord gave to him. As long as Eros, upon which we have already reflected, turns in on itself, it has a tendency toward orgiastic behavior and the unleashing of the passions of the body and of the spirit. Eros demands discipline in order to become fruitful and to be able to expand in a humanizing way. Thus, the formidable abundance of Francis's Eros demanded of him a careful channelization. His balance of Eros was achieved by means of a terrible asceticism. There are many who are scandalized by the inhuman aspects of his austerity. How is it possible that a man so gentle with larks, locusts, the wolf of Gubbio, and all of the creatures of creation could have been so cruel to himself? Saint Bonaventure recounts that "he curbed the stimulus of the senses with a discipline so rigorous that at great pains did he accept what was necessary for his sustenance."[40] He understood his life as a "life of penance" and his order as the Order of Penitents.[41] The meaning of penance should not be sought so much in the extravagances of austerity as in the search for the new man, according to the perspective of *metanoia* in the New Testament. Mortification, as the etymological meaning of the word suggests, lies in the activity of putting to death the overflowing of the passions so that their creative power may be directed toward holiness and humanization. This was the meaning that Francis gave to privations: the subjugation of the body so that it might be faithful to his plan to serve God in a full and radical way. Francis understands very well that the difficulty of the penances constituted the adequate measure of his inner Eros.[42] Because of this, he was very relentless with himself. He was not so with his brothers; on the contrary, "he rejected excessive severity that was not, at the heart, clothed in mercy, nor sprinkled with the salt of discretion."[43] His gestures of acceptance and gentleness with the brothers who were not able to submit themselves to the rigors of penitence are well known; he interrupts his fast and eats with the brother who cried from hunger.[44] He himself establishes norms as to the way to treat the body: "One must discreetly attend to Brother Body so as not to provoke the storms of laziness. Keep from him any occasion of protest, regardless of whether he begins to feel exhausted from staying awake and persevering in reverent prayer. Brother Body might say: 'I am dying of hunger. I can no longer stand the weight of your sacrifice.' But, if he protests in this way after having eaten, realize that the lazy ass needs to be beaten with the rod."[45] One who speaks in this way is free and is beyond penance. Because of this, he has mercy on his own body and speaks to it tenderly: "Cheer up, Brother Ass, and forgive me, because from now on I am going to try to please you, giving ear to your complaints."[46]

Because of this, the penances are at the service of achieving discretion and discipline, without which there cannot be a mature personality. Those who surrender to Eros ought to also apply themselves, like Francis, to the obtaining of discipline with regard to the passions. Francis recognizes that penances carried him to that complete accord between spirit and body, between the desire to ascend and obedience to passionateness. To the little brother who asked him how diligently his body had obeyed him, the saint answered: "Son, I can give witness that it has obeyed me in every way . . . doing what I commanded. . . . We have always been in agreement in this: in following without resistance Christ the Lord."[47] Eros overcomes itself by expanding within the context of some project accepted in total radicalness. The result of the orientation of the passionateness of Eros is gentleness, compassion, the capacity to transcend and live the liberty that is found in the joy of self-determination. Francis achieved, with tremendous effort, this freedom and the splendor of life at its birth, thanks to the rigor of penitence. Here is the secret of the fascination that radiates from his Pathos for life. Francis's penance, apparently so inhuman, was the price he had to pay for his profound humanity. True gentleness is born of strength. This binomial is contained in a small formula at the beginning of the founding text: "The rule and life of the Friars Minor is this. . . ." Life marks the presence of Eros, the explosion of energy, and rule, its ordering and integration. Rule is not meant to substitute for life, but rather to give it strength and form.

Gentleness and Care with the Poor

Francis's gentleness is demonstrated especially in his human relationships. He breaks the rigidity of the feudal hierarchy and calls all persons "brothers and sisters." He himself is called "little brother" (*fratello*).[48] "He wanted to unite great and small, to treat the wise and simple with brotherly affection, to bind with ties of love those who were held at a distance."[49] These are not theoretical expressions, but affective. He treated everyone with utmost courtesy, even Saracens, infidels, and thieves: "Come, brother robbers, we are all brothers and we have some good wine."[50] Thomas of Celano, Francis's first biographer, returns over and over again to the theme of gentleness and affability in Francis's relationships:[51] "He was enchanting . . . in fraternal charity . . . in affection . . . very wise when he gave counsel, always faithful to his obligations."[52] He listened to each person as if he were listening to a great crowd.

He was especially gentle with the poor and the poorest of the poor, the lepers. The biographers are unanimous in stating that Francis's first conversion was toward the poor and crucified, and from them toward the poor and crucified Christ. In his youth, he saved cloth from his father's store for them.[53] Still in the world, "many times, stripping himself of his garments, he dressed the poor with them, those who, if not in fact, in his heart he wanted to be like."[54] After his conversion, the poor and the poor Christ were for him one and the same passion. "The spirit of Francis moved him to the level of the poor, and those he could not help, he showed them his affection."[55] He could not stand for anyone to be poorer than he; he gave away his mantle, a part of his habit, and even all of his clothes, leaving himself naked and exposed to the derision of everyone. The biographer explains the meaning of these gestures: "He suffered to meet someone poorer than he, not because of vainglory, but because of a feeling of true compassion."[56] As is readily seen, tenderness and compassion are at the root of his fundamentally human relations.

However, he was affectionate and gentle in a special way with the least of persons, the lepers. Nothing seemed to him more abominable than the misery of the lepers. His conversion meant a penetration, each time more profound, into this inhuman reality. "The Lord took me among the lepers, and I resorted to mercy among them,"[57] he says in his *Testament*. He began to live with the lepers, caring for them, healing their wounds, feeding them, denying himself so to serve them, even to the point of kissing them on the mouth.[58] The first companions lived among the lepers, dedicated to their service.[59] At the end of his life, in the middle of the crisis in the order, he went back to the affectionate service of these brothers, who constantly made present the suffering servant, Jesus Christ.[60]

His gentleness and care with the poor was so great that he never even permitted himself to think ill of them. For example, we are reminded of the punishment imposed by Francis upon the brother who spoke ill of a poor man. A brother had said to Francis, in front of a poor man, that "his compassion was changed to heartfelt affection." Francis answered him, exasperated: "Brother, it is true that he is a poor man, but there is perhaps no one in the whole region richer than he in desire." And he commanded him to ask forgiveness: "Go right now and removing your tunic, and lying at his feet, beg pardon of him. And not only this, but beg him to pray for you."[61]

This attitude of gentleness and tenderness beyond the pleasure principle is the spring that feeds the truth of human relationships. We do not live only by the bread necessary for survival. We want to live humanly. And to live humanly means to feel the warmth of someone who says to us, in spite of our physical and moral misery: "It is good that you exist, Brother. You are welcome. The sun is also yours, the air is everybody's, and love can unite our hearts." Francis understood very well, with accurate intuition, that transcendence is not enough, that is, the striving upward in search of the ultimate mystery that is called the Father. Transcendence alone does not reveal the total truth of the human being, because it only finds light, the splendor of goodness, absolute positivity, God. It is certainly fullness, but it is not yet integration.

In order to arrive at a fullness of integration it is necessary to have the experience of "trans-descendence," an experience we all fear and reject because we fear facing emptiness, solitude, suffering, and death. And so we do not find full human realization as Christ lived it in his paschal mystery of death and resurrection. Through transdescendence, the individual is open to what is below, thrust toward the shadow of the stigmatized poverty of the bodies of the exploited and leprous. Accepting them with gentleness and tenderness, they are integrated through human sharing, especially by the most intimate sharing, which is the compassionate heart. The individual feels cured of her own pain, because she feels accepted in the human universe. Whoever makes her own the totality of this experience of transcendence and transdescendence, like Francis, will be able, from the depths of her heart, to sing the hymn to all creatures, because she has leaned over them, as over a spring, and has heard them singing.

Gentleness and Compassion through the Passion of God

The discovery by Francis of those crucified throughout history led him to discover the God of the original experience of Christianity, of the crucified Absolute. Only after years of living with the poor and lepers did he hear the voice of the Crucified in San Damiano. His personal charism consisted in his proposing to live with all his soul the way of the Holy Gospel.[62] For Francis, the Gospel is Christ. Christ is its *vestiges* (words and gestures) in its concrete historical condition, *poverty*. Because of this, the expression that crosses all of the first Franciscan writings is *sequi vestigia et paupertatem eius*.[63] The novelty of the Poverello is not in trying to radically live the Gospel. Historical investigations[64] have proven that that ideal was common to the principal spiritual groups of the twelfth and thirteenth centuries. Nor does his newness reside in the following of Jesus (to live based on the experience and central attitudes of Jesus), or in his imitation (reproducing his historical gestures). All of this had been and was being lived by past and contemporary evangelical movements. Francis wanted to reproduce and re-present the life of Jesus. This is the root of his insistence on the literal and the rejection of each and every gloss of the Gospel that was the marrow of his concern. Throughout his life he demonstrated a visible desire to dramatize the mystery of Jesus. Within this context, the calling of his disciples, the celebration of the covenant meal with his own at the end of his life,[65] and the stigmata on Alverna find their adequate expression. Essentially, the imitation is not purely exterior, though this is decisive. The exterior is at the service of an experience of identification with Christ in his humanity.[66] The drama ceases to be only that, and begins to become a life in conformity with the way of Jesus.

And here is where the dimension of compassion and gentleness blossoms in the experience of Francis. In him, as in few Christian mystics, the typical experience of the God of the New Testament blossoms in a most original manner. It does not deal with experiencing the God of mystery, beyond any representation, and so, of the Most High. However, this experience common to religions, to biblical Judaism and all monotheism, is also found, admirably attested to by Saint Francis.[67] But this is not his originality; it is best understood in the mystery of the Incarnation, understood as *kenosis*, the humbling and identification by God with the most despised. Francis rightly intuited that, from the downtrodden and the presence of God in them,[68] one finds the intimate and secret heart of Christianism. What moved him and "made him drunk with love and compassion for Christ"[69] is the fact that God made Himself our brother in poverty and humility: "Oh, how holy and lovely to have such a brother, so pleasant, humble, peaceful, sweet, friendly, and more than anything else, desirable. He gave his life for his sheep and prayed to the Father for us!"[70] As one can see, the adjectives used embrace a powerful mixture of gentleness and cordiality.

Francis's personal experience consists of the encounter with God in the humility of the Incarnation. For him, the mystery of the Incarnation is not represented in the metaphysical formulas of the great christological Councils of Ephesus (325 A.D.) and Chalcedon (451 A.D.), in terms of nature and spirit. The abstract formulations, though correct, do not move anyone, owing to the fact that only the intellect is attracted by them. As we have already said, citing the observations of Pascal and Saint-Exupery: "It is the heart that knows God, not reason"; and "One only sees rightly with the heart; the essential is invisible to the eye." The Incarnation is, for Francis, a mystery of divine sympathy and empathy, as the Greek fathers said. God feels passionately attracted to the interior of human nature. Thus, for Francis, to say God Incarnate is to say God the child who cries, who is nursed, who smiles. It is to concretely represent the life of Jesus in the dusty roads of Palestine; his diatribes against the Pharisees; his sharing with the apostles; his hunger; his thirst; his love for Martha, Mary, and Lazarus; his agony in the Garden of Olives; his surrender on the cross.

What is the human attitude, colored by faith, faced by such a divine reality molded by our insignificance? It is gentleness and compassion. And this is what Saint Francis lived, intensely. Let us listen to what Thomas of Celano says: "Of all the solemnities, he preferred to celebrate with ineffable joy the birth of the child Jesus; he called it the feast of feasts, in which God became a tiny baby, nursed at the breast of a human mother."[71]

Understand, he knows that, in this child, divine and human nature form the unique person of the Word; but what moves him is that the Word was nursed and did everything a child does. God took the breast of Mary, whimpered, was caressed, and fell asleep. This is for Francis an object of compassion and gentleness. When he wanted to recreate the crib, in Greccio, for the first time in history, he said: "I desire to celebrate the memory of the child who was born in Bethlehem, and I want to contemplate in some way with my eyes what he suffered in his infant weakness, how he lay in the manger, and how he was placed between the ox and the ass."[72] And even more, in his desire to recreate, on that day he wanted everyone who owned a donkey or an ox to give them an extra ration, that the brothers eat meat, that even the walls eat meat, but since that is not possible, that they be smeared with meat, as homage to the one who became flesh.[73]

Celano, appealing to the testimony of the friars, states: "The brothers who lived together with him know with what gentleness and tenderness, each and every day, he spoke of Jesus. His mouth spoke from the fullness of his heart, the fountain of illuminated love that filled his whole being bubbling forth."[74]

He thought of the Passion of Jesus Christ with particular gentleness: "He wept bitterly because of the Passion of Christ, which he almost always had before his eyes. Remembering the wounds of Christ, he filled the roads with laments, without finding consolation."[75] A basic experience happened to him while "he was praying, deeply moved,"[76] before the crucifix of San Damiano. When he understood that his mission was to rebuild the Church, which was in a ruinous state, his biographer says: "From then on, a holy compassion for the Crucified was fixed in his soul. And the stigmata were stamped deeply on his heart."[77] Meditation on the Passion of Jesus brought out in him a tender compassion; as Saint Bonaventure says very well, summarizing the basic attitude of the holy founder: "A gentle feeling of compassion transformed him into the one who wanted to be crucified."[78]

As we have already said, compassion ought not be confused with masochism, by which a person is satisfied with the feeling of pain itself. By compassion, identification with the pain of another is sought; it is to feel together with, to suffer in communion. This desire to go out to the interior of the other is characteristic of Eros and Pathos, lived intensely by Francis. He is a cordial man, a man of the heart. That heart, which was under suspicion by his culture and by official Christianity, finds its place in Saint Francis. That heart feels, sings, praises, vibrates, cries, is moved. That heart feels the wound of the other heart. This volcanic force, domesticated nevertheless by penance and the cross, is sensed in everything.

This compassion found its highest expression in the mystic experience of Mount Alverna, three years before the death of Francis. He fasted forty days in the silence of a cave. He desired a radical identification with the Crucified. He asked for two graces, pain and love: "My Lord, Jesus Christ, two graces I ask that you grant me before my death: the first that I experience in my life, in my soul, and in my body that pain that you suffered in the hour of your bitter Passion; the second that I experience in my heart, as much as possible, that measureless love with which you, Son of God, burned when you offered yourself to suffer so much for us sinners."[79] His meditation of the Passion was so intense that "Francis was completely transformed in Jesus through love and compassion."[80] And upon seeing the Crucified in the form of the Seraph, Saint Bonaventure comments: "Francis experienced such compassion that a sword pierced his heart."[81] Through a "mental fire," as the *Fioretti* say, there was produced in Francis the copy of the crucified Christ.[82] And it was then that the whole mountain, according to the symbolic story, also caught fire and "seemed to burn among bright flames that illuminated all of the mountains and valleys around as if the sun shone over the land."[83] In this *beata passio et compassio* the greatest identification of a man with his prototype took place. "Oh, truly Christian gentleman! In his life he tried to conform himself in everything to the living Christ, and in his death he wanted to imitate the dead Christ, and after his death he seemed like the dead Christ. How well he deserved to be honored with such an explicit likeness."[84]

Francis achieved in a magnificent way this ideal of sanctity that comes from "ecstatic emotionality,"[85] from the desire to identify with the other, especially the lesser and most suffering, by way of gentleness and compassion.

Gentleness toward Saint Clare: Integration of the Feminine

Whoever seems to possess a bubbling spring of gentleness will have to extend it to the loved one. How did Francis integrate the feminine in his life? Every man grows and matures beneath the gaze of woman and every woman approaches her adult identity beneath the gaze of man.[86] Within this dialectical relationship the possibilities of gentleness and care are nurtured, without which human life is weakened or hardened. The paths of this integration are the most torturous and dramatic of the human adventure. It was the same way with Francis.

The feminine and the masculine are ontological determinations of every human being, in such a way that each individual carries something of both within him or her self. Man and woman form the difference within human unity, but this difference is not capsulized against the other, but rather is opened in a profound reciprocity. The male must integrate the anima that gives him strength, that is, the dimension of gentleness, of care, of attraction, of intuition, of all that is linked to the mystery of life and generation. The female must integrate the animus that is found within her existence, that is, objectivity of the world, rationality, ordering, and direction—everything that is linked to history. In the difficult balance of these two poles, the one solar and the other lunar, the profile of each human person and the wealth of their depth is built. We find in Francis one of the most joyful syntheses that has been developed in Western Christian culture. There is in him all of the strength of the animus, and at the same time, an extraordinary expansion of the anima. Without machismo or feminism, without fragility or rigidity, there blossoms in him, harmoniously, a gentle strength and a strong gentleness that are the brilliance and archetypal enchantment of his personality.

Francis has a clear consciousness that this liberty to love is not bought without a price. We live in a decadent situation. Passionateness, the seductive power of Eros, illusions of imagination (the person loved is always the person imagined)—all exist. Because of this, a special vigilance and asceticism in the attitudes of Saint Francis come into play. The effort of discipline tries to maintain human stature in a reality that, if on the one hand it ceases to push Eros to the utmost expression of Agape, on the other, it may turn into depravations in the form of domination and obsession.

To understand the gentle relationship between Francis and Clare, it is important to consider the specific meaning of purity that is found in their writings.[87] Evidently, life totally consecrated to God in celibacy and chastity is part of the following of Jesus. There is more to chastity than renouncing marital relationships. For Francis, purity is a synonym for liberty. The only one who is pure is the one who is free of the very attachments of the false absolutes of life: self-promotion, accumulation of prestige, fame, wealth, power, holiness as a personal gain, etc.[88] For Francis, only God is the Highest Good and All Good; He does not allow for any competition of any kind. To find substitutes for God is impurity. To be pure is to be free for the absolute of God. This does not mean that the search for this world's values is deprived of any meaning. It has a finite meaning, and as such, is loved and joyfully sung by Francis. In terms of relationship, man-woman does not mean a split in gentleness and love, but rather their orientation toward a greater love. The man, or the woman, cannot be absolute for the human heart; if it were otherwise, God would not be the first and only. Purity in the mind of Francis is that brothers and sisters love each other in such a way that the love of God grows and may be enjoyed in this world. Only then will the pure see God, especially present in all brothers and sisters.

In the relationship between Francis and Clare, this purity shines in a special way. Between them there is love and relationship of extraordinary gentleness, but, at the same time, a clarity of intentions and a convergence in the love of God, free of any type of suspicion.[89] There is something here of the mysterious, of Eros and Agape, of fascination and transfiguration.[90]

In the legend of Saint Clare, there are explicit references to the mutual attraction between the two while they were still young: Francis already converted and Clare still living in her parents' house.[91] Clare, knowing the reputation of the converted youth, "wanted very much to see him and listen to him."[92] The story continues: "Francis's desire to meet her and speak with her was no less, owing to the prestige of such a gracious girl."[93] Clare visited Francis more often, and "they located the encounters such that their divine friendship was not noted by anyone, nor were they the gossip of the people."[94] Clandestinely, and accompanied by a friend, Clare met Francis. His words "seemed to her to be flaming and his conduct superhuman," language, as can be seen, proper to those in love.

An old legend makes reference to the freshness of this gentle and pure love:

On one occasion there arose some murmurings about the mystic relationship between Francis and Clare. Francis listened to some of these commentaries. He then said to Clare: "Did you hear, Sister, what they are saying about us?" Clare did not answer. She felt as if her heart had been paralyzed and that if she said a word she would begin to cry. "We ought to stay apart," Francis added. "You go ahead and before night falls you will be at the convent. I will go alone, following you, as the Lord has led me to understand." Clare knelt down in the middle of the road. A little while later she recovered, and getting up, she continued on her way, without looking back. The road led into a forest. Suddenly, Clare felt herself fail, without consolation or hope, not being able to say a single word of goodbye to Francis. She waited a few moments and then said: "Father, when shall we see each other again?" "When summer comes again, when the roses bloom," Francis answered. Then something marvelous happened. It was as if over the fields covered with snow there had suddenly opened thousands of multicolored flowers. Overcoming her initial perplexity, Clare leaned over, made a bouquet of roses, and gave it to Francis.

And the legend adds: "And from then on, Francis and Clare were never separated."[95]

We are involved in the symbolic language of legends. But they are what contain the magnificence of the primordial faces of the heart.[96] "Francis and Clare were never separated" means that both were so united in the same evangelical endeavor, so strongly tied to a third reality above and beyond them, the poor Christ, his Gospel, and the service of the poor, that essentially nothing would distance the one from the heart of the other. Both had their heart anchored in God. Because of this, space and time did not count for them. Essentially, as is said in one of the testimonies for the canonization of Clare, Francis communicated to her the very substance of life. "He seemed to her to be gold so clear and brilliant that in him all was reflected as in a mirror."[97]

We know the story. At Francis's request, the young Clare, adorned like a bride, fled her house at night. Francis and his companions waited for her with lighted torches near the Portiuncula. They cut her long blond hair, preserved even today, and "as before the nuptial bed of this virgin, the humble servant was married to Christ" at the hands of Francis.[98] Clare would then, affectionately, call herself "the little plant of the blessed Francis" (*plantula, plantuncula*).[99] Clare was "in love with poverty,"[100] like Francis. He "promised to care for Clare and her sisters as he did his own brothers," [101] as Clare records in her rule.

The love that they had for each other, always excelled by the love of both for the poor and for Christ, made them spiritual twins. When Francis had doubts about his own vocation, he charged Clare and her sisters to pray to God for light.[102] And when she suffered pressures because of the "privilege of radical poverty" (which excluded goods and inheritances) from the pope, Francis also worried with his whole heart.[103] "On one occasion, tired, he came upon a bubbling spring. He sat for a long while, looking at the water. Then he got up, and said to brother Leo: 'Brother Leo, little lamb of God, do you know what I have seen in the depths of the water?' 'The moon, Father, that is reflected there!' 'No, Brother Leo, it was not the moon; by the grace of God I have seen the clear image of our Sister Clare, shining with joy, in such a way that all of my doubts have disappeared.' "

On another occasion, Francis and Clare were eating together at Saint Mary of the Angels, seated on the ground. Suddenly they felt their hearts burning with the love of God. It was then that the inhabitants of the region saw a great light over the house, the church, and the forest, as if they were burning, and ran hastily to put out the flames. Were they not surprised to see Francis and Clare and the brothers in ecstasy, with arms raised toward the sky![104] We are again within the realm of symbolic language: love of the one for the other bursts toward the heavens, toward God, without ceasing to be, in everything, a profoundly human love.

When Francis was close to death, Clare also fell gravely ill. Fearing she would die before him, "she cried inconsolably because she would not be able to see once more her only father after God." And she let Francis know of her affliction. He "was very moved, because he had a father's love for Clare and her sisters."[105] He sent her a note with his blessing, which Clare would include later in chapter six of her rule. Before finishing his famous canticle in praise of all the creatures, "he also dictated a canticle, words and music, to console" Clare and her sisters, because he was filled with "sentiments of piety and love for them."

We know, at the same time, of the affection of Francis for Jacoba de Settesoli, a rich Roman widow, whom he called "Brother Jacoba." Francis liked the honey cakes that she prepared for him very much. He was her guest while in Rome, and he wanted to see her at his death.[106]

This gentle love of Francis, which does not fear the heart, was a realistic and vigilant love, as is seen in the rule,[107] which asks the avoidance of suspicious friendships and vain words in relationships with women. He himself put this into practice. He stopped visiting Clare and her sisters, "not because the affection he felt for them had diminished," but to give an example that "the service to the sisters ought to be exercised only by those who, after much experience, demonstrated that they possessed the Spirit of the Lord."[108]

For Francis, the woman is the path for the love of God and the revelation, in human love, of the very love of God toward humanity. She is not to be a motive for flight or for obsession. With a clean gaze, which dispels the seductions of the imagination, he can look at Clare with chaste love, enriching both of them mutually on the path of their own essential identity.[109]

Gentleness toward the Brothers: Mothers among Themselves

The biographies of his time do not tire of pointing out the gentleness of Francis toward his brothers: "He loved his own brothers in a special way, deeply and with all his heart."[110] In his writings, the word *brother* is used more than any other (242 times), almost always accompanied by an adjective of affection: "my most beloved brothers," "my blessed brothers," "my brothers." His care and tenderness were so intense that he was loved like a "most loved mother."[111] And essentially that is how he acted. Upon seeing Brother Sylvester sick with hunger, he thought to himself: "A few ripe grapes would do this brother a lot of good. And he got up very early in the morning, while the rest were asleep," and he invited him to eat a breakfast of bunches of ripe grapes from a nearby vine.[112] He did the same with Brother Leo, weakened by hunger on the road. He took a few grapes from a vine close to the road and offered them to him, which cost him a few blows from the owner. But the brother was revived.[113]

He asked in his rule that the brothers have the same tenderness and care for the others: "Each one love and feed his brother like a mother loves and cares for her child."[114] In the Rule for Hermitages he says that the brothers who live in the hermitages should not number more than three or, at most, four: "Two are to be mothers, and have two children, or at least, one," and "the children at times will take the office of mothers."[115] "Admirable compassion and gentleness"[116] he showed to the sick, and in a special way he had "unique patience and gentleness"[117] with those in anguish (we would say neurotic), considering them to be as fragile as babies. The brothers were not only brothers; Francis wanted them to be "lesser brothers," that is, "subject to all,"[118] at the service of one and all, "centering all their affection on the community."[119]

This attitude of care causes the energies of humanization to overcome the tendencies toward smallness and isolation that also play a part in human life together. Life together aids the expansion of Eros, as Celano reflects admirably and in an idealized way: "When they were found together in some place, or when, as happened, they were found on the road, worthy of poetry was the spiritual love that blossomed between them, and now they displayed a true affection, superior to any other love. Love that was manifested in chaste embraces, in gentle affections, in holy kisses, in pleasant conversation, in modest smiles, in festive faces, in simple gazes, in humble attitudes, in guarded tongues, in calm answers; they were united in the ideal, diligent in service, untiring in works."[120]

Confraternization with Nature: The Cosmic Democracy

All of the oldest biographies of Saint Francis are in agreement in affirming "the friendly union that he established with all things."[121] The first of the biographers, Thomas of Celano (1229), testifies:

> Who can explain the joy that arose in his spirit from the beauty of the flowers, contemplating the gallantry of their shapes and the breathing of the fragrance of their aromas? . . . And finding himself in the presence of many flowers, he preached to them, inviting them to praise the Lord, as if they enjoyed the gift of reason. And he did the same thing with fields and vineyards, with rocks and forests, and with all of the beauty of the countryside, the waters of the springs, the fruits of the orchards, land and fire, air and wind, inviting them with genuine purity to divine love and to joyful fidelity. Finally, he called all creatures his brothers and sisters, like one who had arrived at the glorious freedom of the children of God.[122]

The whole universe surrounding Saint Francis is surrounded by infinite gentleness and of "the most gentle feeling of devotion toward all things"; [123] "he felt as if transported by a heartfelt love by all creatures." [124] Because of this, he walked with reverence over rocks, in considerations of the One who Himself is called Rock; he gathered the worms in the road so that they would not be stepped on by the travelers; he provided the bees with honey and wine in the winter so that they would not perish from hunger and cold. [125]

Here is made clear a distinct way of being-in-the-world, not over things, but together with them, like brothers and sisters of the same family. To his own agonies and sufferings "he gave not the name of pains but of brothers." [126] Death itself was for him a friend and a sister. Because of this, the Franciscan world is full of magic, of reverence, of respect. It is not a dead and inanimate universe; things are not tossed here, within the reach of possessive appetites of hunger; nor are they placed one beside another. They are alive and have their own personality; they have blood ties with humanity; they live in the same Father's house as humanity. And because they are brothers and sisters, they cannot be violated, but rather must be respected. It is from this that Saint Francis, surprisingly, but consistent with his nature, prohibits the brothers from cutting any tree at the roots, that they might bud again. He commanded the gardeners to leave a plot of uncultivated land so that all types of grasses might grow (including weeds), because "they too proclaim the beauty of the Father in all things." [127] He also wanted, in the orchards, together with the vegetables and fruit trees, flowers and aromatic herbs to be grown "so that all who contemplate them may be drawn to eternal sweetness." [128]

The Marriage of Eros and Agape

How did Saint Francis arrive at this intimate sympathy with all things? In the first place, because he was a great poet, not romantic but ontological, that is, a poet capable of capturing the transcendent and sacramental message that all things send out. In his youth he was influenced by the erotic Provençal movement. [129] He sang songs of love and admiration for the beauty of the ladies. As we have already said, Eros is at the root of the Franciscan experience of universal fraternity. But it is an Eros purified of the weight of the material and of all ambiguity of the French gallantries aimed at enchanting women, by its interpenetration by Agape. Agape, Christian love, does not crush Eros; nor does it sublimate it; rather, it radicalizes its basic impulse until it reaches the foundation and fascination of all love, which is God giving Himself in and through all things.

Conversion does not repress the erotic movement, but rather purifies it. Francis's love for Clare maintained all of the intensity of love, though free of the strings of the libido; it is a love transfigured by the fascination for the mystery that resides in each person. This interior movement led Francis to personalify all of his relationships: poverty is not poverty but Lady Poverty; the virtues are not virtues but Queen Wisdom, her holy sister Pure Simplicity; the lark is not a lark but Sister Lark; similarly, Brother Wolf, Lord Brother Sun, Mother and Sister Earth. Because he was able to purify love of all inner evil, he could, until the end of his life and even in the hour of his death, sing the songs of love he learned in his childhood. He liked to call himself God's troubador.

However, recourse to the poetic soul of Francis does not explain adequately the depth of his experience of being-with-things as brothers and sisters of the same household. At the root of it all, there is the religious experience of the universal fatherhood of God. The paternity of God was not for Francis a cold dogma and a conclusion of the rationalist as to the contingency of creatures. It was a profound emotional experience; it meant a cosmic identification with all the elements. The truth of the universal fatherhood of God is the nucleus of the message of Jesus. The Christian tradition always proclaimed this truth; but the first to live it with this dimension of emotion, with all creatures felt as brothers and sisters, was without a doubt Francis of Assisi.

Until Saint Francis, God the Father was traditionally considered the great lord of the cosmos. The creatures were thought of in terms of their radical dependence on this one principle. He lived the filial character of all beings, not only of humanity and much less of only the baptized. The individual, as child in the Son Jesus Christ, shared in the cosmic lordship of the Great Father. Humanity was considered lord of creation, above all things, without being subject to any of them. It was the landlord of God the Father. It prolonged within the world the vertical relationship that was born in God, passed through humanity, and reached the creatures. The mysticism of universal sonship was thus lived out.

The novelty of Francis consists in the living of the horizontal dimension: if all are children of God, all are brothers and sisters to one another. All live in the same Great House of the Father. All acquire a deep intimacy with all things. Enemies do not exist. No one threatens us. We are enveloped in an atmosphere of love for brothers and sisters. The two movements are found in Saint Francis: horizontal and vertical. Thomas of Celano and Saint Bonaventure emphasize this very well: "He admired in every thing its Author and in all events he recognized the Creator. . . . In all things beautiful he recognized the One who is Beauty and whatever was good caused him to shout: 'The one who has made us is the best.' He followed the Beloved everywhere with the footprints imprinted in all things, and with all things he made a stairway by which he ascended to His throne." But he did not remain only in that dimension: "He was filled with a greater gentleness when he thought of the first and common origin of all beings, and he called all creatures, no matter how small they were, by the name of brother or sister, because he knew that they all had in common with him the same beginning."[130]

With what emotion do we read Francis's scolding of Brother Fire when, almost blind, he needed to be operated on, or rather, cauterized with a red-hot iron from the ear to the eyebrow: "Fire, my brother, the Most High has created you strong, beautiful, and useful, giving you a dazzling presence, which all other creatures envy. Be kind and courteous to me in this trance. I beg the Lord to cause you to temper your strength, so that by burning me gently I may tolerate you."[131] And Brother Fire, the story adds, had mercy on Francis.

That fraternity places Francis on the same level as the creatures. He does not define himself as distinct from them, by emphasizing what makes him different and so distancing himself from the brothers.

When he sings, he does it with all creatures, as is said in his wonderful "Canticle of Brother Sun." He does not sing alone through the creatures. It would be selfish to become deaf to the hymn that they themselves sing to the Creator. He sings with them, with the cricket,[132] and with the lark: "The sister larks praise their Creator. Let us go among them and sing ourselves to the Lord, reciting his praises and the canonical hours."[133]

Modern humanity has difficulty singing along with things because we are not with them. Because of this, we cannot hear their essential ballad. Saint Francis is closer to a Cézanne or a Van Gogh than to a Picasso or a Di Cavalcanti. These project their subjectivity onto things that reflect human feelings. The "dead" things of nature—the table, the bowl of fruit, the water pitcher—are there, in their own light, in great humility, without any human projection. They sing to God for the fact of being what they are. Saint Francis, archaic and unmodern man, unites himself with this silent song, letting things be what they are, brothers and sisters too adorable to be manipulated by brother humanity.

The Nonromanticism of Saint Francis

A great deal of the fascination about Saint Francis today comes from his love for nature. It was during the European age of romanticism that the singular figure of Saint Francis was discovered. But he is not an *avant la lettre* romantic.[134] Romanticism is characterized by modern subjectivity; it is the projection onto the world of feelings themselves. For the modern romantic, nature points consciousness back toward itself, to its feelings, but not toward the hearing of the message that arises from nature, which points to something beyond consciousness: the mystery of God. In romanticism, the *I* remains in its own universe, rich, with varied emotions, but closed in on itself. In an archaic way of thinking like that of Saint Francis, the *I* is urged to rise above itself, to open its closed circle, and to become a brother or sister with all things to sing together a hymn of praise to the Great Father of us all.[135] But this is only possible by means of a profound asceticism and an interrupted effort at purification and denial of the desire for the possession and domination of things.

We have previously reflected upon the poetic structure of the soul of Saint Francis and his religious experience of the universal fatherhood of God, source of the fraternity of all beings. The analysis would be insufficient if we did not insist on another aspect, perhaps the most essential of all: Francis's radical poverty.[136]

His experience of universal fraternity, as we have already said and continue to underscore, was not the result of a rational argument about the fatherhood of God. It was a basic and vital experience. How does one articulate this experience within which universal fraternity was manifested? We believe that in the answer to this question is the intimate secret of Saint Francis's archaic way of being. The poetic structure of the Franciscan soul and of Christian faith are indispensable ways of understanding his way of being; the key, however, is not to be found there, but rather in a new praxis of Saint Francis. At a definite moment in his youth he is converted. As in every authentic conversion, a *conversio morum* takes place, a change in the way of behaving and relating.[137] A break occurs. One world dies and another is born. Francis began to identify himself with the poor and to do difficult penances. A painful process of interior purification was begun. He retired to the caves; long vigils; fasts and penances so rigorous that he had to be merciful to his own body, which he tenderly called Brother Ass. The core of this effort at interiorization centered around the theme of poverty. Poverty, fundamentally, does not only consist in not having things, because individuals always have things: their body, their intelligence, their clothes, their being-in-the-world. Poverty is a way of being by which the individual lets things be what they are; one refuses to dominate them, subjugate them, and make them the objects of the will to power. One refuses to be over them in order to be with them. This demands an immense asceticism of the renunciation of the instinct to power, to the dominion over things, and to the satisfaction of human desires. Poverty is the essential path of Saint Francis, realized in the physical place of the poor. The poorer he was, the freer and more fraternal he felt. Possession is what engenders the obstacles to communication between human beings themselves and between persons and things. Interests, selfishness, and exclusive possessions interfere between the individual and the world. They are placed at a distance and a well of alienating objectifications is sunk between them. The more radical the poverty, the closer the individual comes to reality, and the easier it is to commune with all things, respecting and reverencing their differences and distinctions. Universal fraternity is the result of the way-of-being-poor of Saint Francis. He truly felt a brother because he could gather all things devoid of the interest in possessions, riches, and efficiency. Poverty is thus a synonym for humility; this is not another virtue, but an attitude by which the individual is on the ground, in the earth, at the side of all things. Converting oneself to this way of being, and in the measure of its realization, one is rewarded with the transparence of all things to the divine and transcendent reality. In this way, universal reconciliation and a cosmic democracy is achieved.

Saint Bonaventure came to affirm that Saint Francis, "through the friendly union that he established with all things, seemed to have returned to the primitive state of original innocence."[138] This was the result of his complete disownment, after a long and demanding novitiate. Finally, he revived in his heart the earthly paradise in the calm brotherhood of all beings, children of the same Father and brothers and sisters to each other. Only through a process of interior purification and denial of the world could he regain the world, in a truly fraternal way.

Whoever tries to romantically imitate Saint Francis in his love for nature without passing through asceticism, denial, penitence, and the cross falls into a deep illusion. The world will soon discover the individual's sadness and will show him or her their contradictions. Only he or she is able, without falling into empty words, to call fire one's brother destroyer, water a humble and chaste sister, the agony of illness and death one's sister who, by means of an arduous penance and a profound stripping, has removed all of the obstacles placed between the individual and all creatures. It was at the end and not at the beginning of his life that Francis composed the hymn to Brother Sun. To begin where Francis ended is a disastrous illusion. Making the effort to retrace the path, in great humility, trying to become one with things, especially the smallest, is to feed the hope that perhaps our world may also be transformed and may reveal its fraternal and filial character.

The Synthesis of Interior Archaeology and Exterior Ecology

Saint Francis's way-of-being-with-things resulted in a total reconciliation of a man with his universe. There exists in the human heart a secret and persistent call to a fullness of salvation and life, to complete fraternization with all things and universal unity with the most distant and different realities, such as God and death.

The principle of hope and the dimension of the utopic that structurally mark the spirit have populated the human mind, in all ages, with dreams of a reconciliation like this one. In Saint Francis, the utopic became topic, made history of the actuality of the sweetness of the fraternity with all things. The intimate archaeology was reconciled with exterior ecology by means of a deep diving into the mystery of God. In the "Canticle of Brother Sun" we find the testimony to this precious synthesis.[139]

THE ARCHETYPAL SACRAMENTALITY OF THE CANTICLE ELEMENTS

There are many ways of reading the "Canticle of Brother Sun." The first and most common takes into account the poetic character of the text; it relies on the named elements, such as the sun, the earth, the stars, fire, water, and death. Through them, the mystic Francis is elevated toward God. This tendency is inscribed in the writings of the great poet mystics, from the psalms to John of the Cross, Teresa of Avila, and also Teilhard de Chardin.[140] This interpretation is valid, but does it reveal all of the richness contained in the canticle?

There is another type of reading that descends to a deeper and more structural level, plumbing the archetypal subconsciousness of the psyche of the poet-mystic. The elements of the canticle preserve their material reality, are not allegorized, but acquire for the mystic a symbolic value, expressive of a state of the soul. They are the vehicle by which the poet tries to express what happens in the intimacy of his being: the religious-mystic union of everything with God. This is the path we propose to follow, briefly, to analyze the poem of Saint Francis.

The knowledge of the context within which this text arose will help us to understand better the advantage of this archeological and archetypal analysis. The legend of Perugia[141] has given us the most detailed account. Close to twenty years had passed since his conversion and two years since the stigmatization on Alverna. The saint was being consumed by seraphic love, "an undying dying,"[142] to use Saint Bonaventure's expression, and he was visited by every kind of internal and external suffering. He was almost blind. He saw that the order he had founded was following paths that threatened the living out of radical poverty; the Church had organized Crusades against the Saracens, whom he himself had visited in the Orient, becoming scandalized at the barbarity of the Christians. It was the autumn of 1225. Saint Clare and the rest of the sisters were living at San Damiano, the little chapel where everything had begun. The suffering gave Francis no relief. Fifty days passed, according to the legend, closed in a dark cell, not able to see the sun during the day or the fire at night. His suffering did not allow him to sleep or even rest. "One night when he felt more weighed down than usual by many painful troubles, he began to feel sorry for himself within his heart." Celano adds that, then, Francis faced a fierce struggle to overcome his pains and impatience. *"Orans . . . sic positus in agone . . ."*: thus praying, he entered into agony. In that trance, he heard in his spirit a voice that said to him: "Tell me, Brother, would you not be happy were someone to give you as a recompense for your sufferings and tribulations a treasure so great and precious that neither the entire earth turned into gold, nor rocks into precious stones, nor water into balsam would be of comparable value?" And the blessed Francis answered: "Lord, it would be a priceless treasure, and greatly desirable." "Well then," said the voice, "be happy, Brother, and joyful in the midst of your tribulations and illness, because they are gifts of my kingdom, and you may be assured you are destined for it."[143]

In that moment, Francis's spirit overflowed with joy. His dark night was transformed into day, feeling already within the Kingdom of God, which is the symbol of total reconciliation, of the overcoming of all contradictions, and the greatest realization of humanity with the cosmos and with God. He got up, meditated a few moments, and began to sing the hymn of all creatures: *Altissimu, omnipotente, bon Signore. . . .* He called the brothers and sang with them the hymn he had just composed. This canticle of light arose in the midst of a dark night of the body and soul. It emerged from the depths of an existence that was blossoming, though suffering and troubled, like a shoot that untiringly searches from within the trunk the light of the sun. It is the expression of a reconciled universe that was taking shape within the heart of Francis.

It does not deal only with a poetic-religious discourse on all things: the things themselves seem to be involved in a much deeper discourse. The cosmic praise unveiled the subconscious symbolic language of an interior itinerary, an unveiling of the depths of the soul; it was presented, more exactly, like a poetic reconciliation of the man with his archeology, an opening of himself to the totality of an existence in the light of being.[144] The sun continues to be the sun; fire, fire; water, water. But beyond their objective value, these elements also have a symbolic worth. Humanity expresses by means of these elements its interior world. And what does that interior world express? It expresses the emergence of universal reconciliation, the fusion between the cosmic mysticism, oriented toward fraternity with nature, and evangelical mysticism, oriented toward love for the person of Christ. The elements praised in the canticle gain an archetypal sacramentality, communicating this fusion.

Canticle of Brother Sun

Altissimu, omnipotente, bon Signore,
 tue so'le laude, la gloria e l'honore
 et onne benedictione:

Ad te solo, Altissimo, se konfano
 et nullu omo ene dignu
 te mentovare.

Laudato sie, mi'Signore, cum tucte le tue creature,
 spetialmente messor lo frate sole,
 lo cualle iorno et allumini noi per loi;

Et ellu è bellu e radiante
 cum grande splendore:
 de te, Altissimu, porta significatione.

Laudato si', mi'Signore, per sora luna e le stelle;
 in celu l'ài formate clarite
 et pretiose et belle.

Laudato si', mi'Signore, per frate vento
 et per aere et nubilo et sereno et onne tempo,
 per lo quale a le tue creature dai sustentamento.

Laudato si', mi'Signore, per sora aqua,
 la quale è multo utile et humile
 et pretiosa et casta.

Laudato si', mi'Signore, per frate focu
 per lo quale annallumini la nocte;
 ed ello è bello et iocundo et robustoso et forte.

Laudato si', mi'Signore, per sora nostra matre terra,
 la quale ne sustenta et governa
 et produce diversi fructi con coloriti fioro et herba.

Laudato si', mi'Signore,
   per quelli ke perdonano per lo tuo amore,
   et sostengo' infirmitate et tribulatione;

Beati quelli kei sosterrano in pace,
   ka da te, Altissimo,
   sirano incoronati.

Laudato si', mi'Signore,
   per sora nostra morte corporale,
   da la qualle nullu homo viventi po skappare:

Guai acquelli ke morrano ne le peccata mortali;
   beati quelli ke trovarà ne le tue sanctissime voluntati,
   ka la morte secunda nol farrà male.

Laudate et benedicite mi'Signore, et rengratiate
   et serviateli cum grande humilitate.

THE COSMIC MARRIAGE THAT IT INSPIRES

It takes a great modern scholar of Saint Francis, Eloi LeClerc,[145] to demonstrate with the resources of the depth of psychologist C. G. Jung, the method of poetic analysis of Gaston Bachelard, and the hermeneutic of Paul Ricoeur how all of the elements of the hymn to Brother Sun possess a rich archetypal content in order to express the experience of total reconciliation achieved by the saint.

The structure of the canticle reveals this archetypal expression of unity. The seventh strophe unconsciously discovers this search. Seven is formed by adding three and four, which are the greatest symbols of totality and unity. In the number seven, two lines cross—the vertical and the horizontal—which together also form a recognized symbol of totality. The first movement is directed vertically toward God: "Most high, all powerful and good Lord . . ." Francis immediately realizes that he cannot sing to God, because "no one is worthy of making mention of You." But he does not become bitter over this. He returns, horizontally, to the creatures: "Praise to you, my Lord, for all your creatures." He opens himself to universal fraternity and sings to the creatures, not in themselves, but as marked by the experience of the Most High who made it possible to see them as sacraments of God: "Because from You, Most High, they are meaningful."

Another archetypal symbol of the psychic totality of the human person runs throughout the hymn: the masculine and the feminine. All of the elements are ordered in pairs, which combine the masculine and the feminine: sun-moon, wind-water, fire-earth. All of these pairs appear to surround the great marriage of Earth-Sun, from whose cosmic union are born the other couples. He begins by singing to Lord and Brother Sun, archetypal symbol of virility and all paternity, and he concludes with the praise for Mother and Sister Earth, archetype of the feminine and all fecundity. This representation does not translate the objective order of the world, but rather the order of profound meaning. Through it, the most radical subconscious, in its thirst for unity and totality, finds adequate expression.

The hymn also contains two stanzas that were added afterward by the saint. In one of them, the peace attained by Saint Francis between the bishop of Assisi and the mayor is celebrated. The other was inspired shortly before the *transitus* of Saint Francis, in the first days of October of 1226. In both, it is not the material cosmos that is chanted, but the human cosmos, inserted in the grand universal fraternity, attained through tension and suffering. Saint Francis wanted to add them to the original canticle. The truth is that they were born from the same fundamental inspiration. The hymn tries to celebrate the mystical irruption of unity and fraternity with all things and with God. He could not leave out humanity, in its tribulation. The individual is reconciled with other persons. He is reconciled, also, with death, accepting mortal existence. He integrates death with life, accepting it as a sister, or better yet, Francis becomes a brother to death. She thus becomes a symbol of new life and of greater love.[146]

The splendor of humanity and its tragedy—its desire to ascend and its rooting in the earth, its uranic (heavenly) dimension and its telluric (earthly) dimension—find a privileged interpreter in the poor man of Assisi.

The Celebration of the Reconciled Man

Saint Francis's way of being together with his being-with led him to a confraternization with all strata of reality: superior (the Most High God), interior (intimate archeology), and exterior (ecological reality). What unfolds is praise to mystery. Modern humanity, with its being-over is not simply condemned to relate in a dominative way with nature; there is no doubt that we must organize the systematic satisfaction of our basic needs and humanize the world. But we will have to learn a use of our technical power that will be capable of opening us to the deeper and more archetypal dimension of nature. To cultivate the land and experience the fact that she is a generous mother is one thing; to treat her without respect and veneration is quite another. It is one thing to extract her riches and taste her fertility; it is another to abuse and waste her. It is one thing to use the forest; it is another to tear it down indiscriminately.[147]

Modern humanity has forgotten that in our activity with nature we must deal not only with things, but also with something that affects us at our deepest level. We do not simply live in the world. We colive; we become lovers or enemies; we accept or reject. A give and take develops between the interior world and the exterior. We cannot achieve our identity while denying a friendly and fraternal relationship with our natural world. This does not mean an anachronistic romanticism, but rather a right understanding of the basic structure of humanity, to-be-in-the-world-with-all-things, as we have said, in a cosmic democracy.

The Franciscan experience is the historicizing of this truth-reality. In spite of the ruptures that trials may introduce, despite the ultimate solitude that is the meaning of death, it is capable of opening one to universal fraternity, and to singing, not just calling, to all creatures as brothers and sisters. "The mystery of the earth is one with the mystery of the stars." Human praise is one with the essential praise that all things chant to our Creator. Finally, the reconciled individual celebrates the world as a paradise, because he himself or she herself was transformed: "Bless and praise my Lord, and give Him thanks, serving Him in great humility."

CONCLUSION: THE EXEMPLARY QUALITY OF THE SOUL'S EXPANSION

As can be seen from this reflection, our present-day culture finds in Francis a great deal of that for which we hunger and thirst. The expansion of the dimension of the anima in terms of gentleness, care, and living together answers a collective demand of our age in agony. A clear path is left where Francis directed his attention, a path strewn with affection, enthusiasm, and tremendous goodness toward all creatures, especially toward the disinherited of society. For Francis, the small happiness of our troubled existence sinks its roots in the heart of the Father of infinite goodness, but also in a human heart capable of compassion and emotion. Nourished by these two roots, existence is made happy with a finite joy, foretasting already what the Father has prepared for all in His Kingdom. If we do not approach the Father, life becomes empty and existence insupportable. If we do not give ear to the heart and its needs, everything remains sterile and dark. Without the Father, the heart remains barren. Without the heart, the Father has no warmth.

Preferential Option for the Poor

THE MESSAGE OF SAINT FRANCIS
FOR CONTEMPORARY SOCIETY

A legend from the Franciscan tradition recounts that, one day, Francis was very happy because he was beginning to enjoy God in all things. He went out into the streets singing and inviting others to join him in his song. He came upon an almond tree, and he said to it: "Brother Almond, speak to me of God." The almond tree shivered lightly, as if shaken by a gentle breeze, and it blossomed suddenly as if spring had burst forth in it.

Francis continued on his way, even happier. He passed by a creek that had backed up in a cool shaded area. Drunk with the love of God, Francis begged the creek: "Brother Creek, speak to me of God." And the still waters began to bubble as if they were trying to speak. Then they became quiet until they became a mirror of crystal-clear water. Francis gazed intently into the depths of the waters. And he saw in their depths the face of his beloved Clare. He continued on the road, radiant with joy.

A little farther on, he saw some birds perched on a branch. "Little birds, my brothers," he said, "speak to me of God." And the little birds began to chirp in a melody such as had never been heard in that region. Then they became silent; they left the tree, and forming a cross, flew toward heaven like an arrow.

Francis continued on the road, redoubled in joy. And he met a pilgrim, with his knapsack on his back, as if he had been walking for a long time. Francis said to him: "Brother, speak to me of God." And the pilgrim, without saying a word, took Francis by the hand

and took him to the city. They crossed from one part of the city to another, arriving at the place where the poor lived. They went to a plaza, where the women were in line to take water to their houses, while others were washing in the waters of a fountain, older men were sunning themselves, and the children were playing. The pilgrim sat down on a dilapidated bench, opened his knapsack, and began to distribute bread among the children and women. All ate the bread until they were full—men, women, and children. The bread was passed from hand to hand and was miraculously multiplied. Then the pilgrim raised his eyes to heaven and said "Our Father." And then, looking around, he added: "Our bread." Francis understood, and his joy was uncontainable, because he met God in the sharing of bread among the poor and needy brothers who, in turn, shared it among themselves.

———————

The relevance of Saint Francis becomes more patent if we realize the great challenges that modern society brings to us. We will consider, specifically, one of the innumerable challenges that are before us, that which originates from the brutal poverty to which millions and millions of human beings are subjected. A fearful abyss separates humans into classes and nationalities: on the one hand, the great majority struggle on levels of survival in the midst of misery, hunger, illiteracy, and contempt; on the other, a minority enjoy the benefits of prosperity, taking advantage of goods and services.[1] This situation is deteriorating, as the bishops meeting in Puebla (1979) recognized: "A deafening cry rises from millions of persons, asking their shepherds for a liberation that does not come to them from anywhere else. . . . The cry is clear, growing, impetuous, and in some cases, threatening."[2]

POVERTY DEHUMANIZES RICH AND POOR ALIKE

Poverty as the lack of means to produce and reproduce life with a minimum of human dignity is the most painful and bloody wound in the history of humanity. All of the so-called "historical" civilizations of which we have knowledge are characterized by penury and inequality. This stigma, instead of lessening, is aggravated by the methods of capitalistic production by private, elitist, and exclusive ownership. Humanity enjoys more than enough technology to overcome this chronic illness. Together with technological-scientific advances, there has developed a sharp consciousness of the inviolable sacredness of the human person. In spite of this, there is an impasse that results from politico-cultural factors linked to the meaning of life crystallized in the system of modernism, nationalism, domination, and repression of the capitalist world. Meanwhile, levels of misery have reached such an extreme that a worldwide anthropological catastrophe is not impossible. The starving of the world could take over the plazas of all the cities of the world and do vindictive justice such as those of which history has shown us some horrendous precedents: a destruction of the iniquitous without hope of reconstruction upon other foundations of a more just and more human world.[3]

The perplexity and the feeling of guilt before such massive poverty grows in the measure in which we better know the mechanisms that cause it. It is not fate; it is not a demand of nature; it is not the will of God that there be rich and poor.[4] The cause lies in "definite economic, social, and political situations and structures" that, operating on an international level, give rise to the "rich getting richer and the poor becoming poorer."[5]

Poverty is not only a problem of the moral conscience; it is fundamentally a political problem. Because of this, it is not enough to morally condemn situations of poverty; rather a concrete effort must be made to overcome it by means of a true revolution in the arena of the relations between human beings and the means of producing the goods necessary to guarantee the lives of all people.[6] This is the great challenge of the poor to all present-day societies.

The struggle in favor of the poor and of the poor themselves against poverty implies an honest search for the humanization of all. Poverty dehumanizes rich and poor alike. In the first place, the poor: poverty carries with it all kinds of needs; it destroys emotional life, one's relationships with others; it continually places obstacles in the way of the essential vocation of human beings to develop themselves and expand their abilities beyond the survival instinct; it leads them to envy, hatred, violence against those responsible for their misery, and often, against God, raising their fist against heaven.

It dehumanizes the rich because it leads them to consider the poor as inferior, outcasts of society, the dead weight of history. In those societies where there was slavery, there was a brutal dehumanization of the poor. The owner treated those "wretches" as if they were objects to be used, like merchandise; they were, literally, wood for the process of production;[7] it was not uncommon for slaves to have only five to seven years of a useful life, to such an extent were they exploited. Today's dominant classes, successors to the slave owners as well as the slave traders (English, Portuguese, Dutch, and North American), have inherited a profound scorn for the poor. They consider them to be socially disqualified; they avoid contact with them, going around them, insensitive to their misery. The governments controlled by these dominant classes, brutalized in their human emotions, leave to one side the poor who constitute the majority (of our Latin American peoples) in their economic, cultural, urban, and health plans. Any organization and movement of the poor is immediately controlled and repressed with a violence intolerable even to animals.[8] Both sides live full of fear; the poor because of the continuous threats against them and the rich because of the fear of the vindictive rebellion of the poor. The relationship is fraternal, and society is organized on principles of equality and justice only in a euphemistic way.

Saint Francis's option for the poor covers, in this context, an unusual political reality. What makes the poor poorer is the fact of generally being considered from the point of view of the rich. The greatness of Saint Francis consisted in seeing the poor with the eyes of the poor, allowing him, thusly, to discover the values of the poor. Before beginning to analyze this, let us take a quick glance at the attitude of the Church throughout the centuries toward the challenge of the poor.

CHURCH OF THE POOR, FOR THE POOR, WITH THE POOR

We understand the word *poor* in an immediate and direct sense: poor is that individual who is objectively affected by some lack, be it within the social condition (poor businessman, poor professor), be it related to another's condition (economically powerful and economically weak). Michel Mollat, the renowned scholar on the historical phenomenon of poverty, defines the poor in this way:

> He is the one who temporarily or permanently finds himself in a situation of weakness, dependence, humiliation, characterized by the lack of means, variables according to the age and society,

means of power and social consideration: money, relationships, influence, power, science, technical qualifications, honorable birth, physical strength, intellectual ability, personal freedom, and dignity. Living day to day, the poor man has no possibility of changing his state without the help of another. A definition like this one could include all those who are frustrated through their own fault, the asocial, the marginated; this definition is not specific to an age, to a region, or to an environment. Nor does it exclude those who, because of an ascetic or mystic ideal, reject the world, or those who, through devotion, choose to live poverty among the poor.[9]

As we will see later, the poor are defined in terms of relationship, because there are no rich or poor in themselves. In an economic sense, poor (*pauper*) is in opposition to rich (*dives*); in a political sense, poor (*minor, impotens*) is opposed to powerful (*potens, maior*); in a hygienic sense, poor (*infirmus, esuriens, famelicus, vulneratus, debilis*) is distinct from healthy (*sanus*); in a cultural sense, the poor are illiterate (*imbecillis, simplex, idiota*) as opposed to educated; and so on. As is evident, the concept of poor must be wide to adequately capture the phenomenon, which is multidimensional.

How has the Church faced this dehumanizing situation? As diverse as the situations, strategies, and tactics have been, the Church (community of believers) has always had a great concern for the poor. They were always a thorn in its consciousness and an invitation to lend a hand. In essence, the Church has been faithful to the tradition of Jesus Christ, who made an option for the poor, although in a sociological sense it was not poor;[10] it has been faithful also to the apostolic tradition,[11] which in the beginning identified conversion to the Gospel with social conversion, placing "all of the goods in common, sharing them with all, according to the needs of each one, not having any poor among them" (cf. Acts 2:44–45; 4:34). Their care of the poor was always an ecclesial and apostolic concern. It is an unresolved question, but it never fell into an attitude of resignation and inactivity. Something was always done for the poor in the Church.[12]

A Church of the Poor

The primitive Church, until the fourth century, with the advent of the age of Constantine (313 A.D.), was made up largely of the poor. The content of Jesus' message, promising first the Kingdom and salvation to the poor, calling them blessed (Lk 6:20) and the Father's privileged ones (Mt 11:25–26), reached out to meet the religious and social demands of the poor, thus favoring the spread of rising Christianity.[13] The following words of Paul are historical truth: "Brothers, remember that God has called you in spite of the fact that few of you are wise according to human standards, or that few of you are powerful or members of important families. . . . God has chosen those whom the world considers fools, despised and unimportant in this world" (1 Cor 1:26–29). The same situation of the poverty of the first Christians is attested to by the Letter to Diognetus (around the year 50).[14] Christianity did not introduce social transformations, nor was it in a position to do so; but it deeply humanized human relationships, dignifying the poor and placing them on a level of equality and respect among other people.

Very soon, on the other hand, the question of wealth was raised, now that the Church wanted to facilitate the conversion of the rich. The demands of Jesus to sell everything and give it to the poor (cf. Mt 19:16–22 = Mk 10:17–22 = Lk 18:18–27; Lk 12:33–34) are spiritualized in an ascetic and moral perspective according to Saint James and Saint Paul: wealth may be a means of charity and assistance to the poor, and this is justified and legitimated (2 Cor 8:13–14; 1 Tm 6:16–19).

In spite of this historical translation of the radicalness of Jesus, there was always preserved in the ancient Church the reference to the "communism of love" (Ernst Troeltsch) lived by the first Christians in Jerusalem (Acts 2:42–46; 4:32–37). Although the majority were poor, and the Church was presented openly as a community of the poor, the collective poverty was tempered by solidarity, mutual compassion, and charitable assistance.

A Church for the Poor

Beginning with Constantine and Theodosius, the Church is led to accept the hegemonic spread of Western culture. This implies taking the place of political power. From a base, the Church is transformed into a cupola, introducing a division between the simple faithful (*plebs christiana*), who continue to be the base, and the ecclesiastical hierarchy, who are transformed into a body of dignitaries (*nobiles*), the cupola.

In order to carry out its new historical function, the hierarchy allied itself with the powerful of society and the state. From this coalition between church and state (and the dominant classes represented in it) is born the historical-cultural phenomenon called "Christianity."[15] Christianity resulted from the alliance between the *sacerdotium* and the *imperium*. Within this structuring, the poor (at the same time Christian) find themselves below and at the margin. But they have never been forgotten. Essentially, the strategy of the hierarchical Church is conditioned by the place of power that it occupies. The poor will almost always be seen, though with notable exceptions, from the perspective of the rich. And so the poor always seem inferior, in need, and the object of charitable activity. The politico-pastoral strategy will take the form of aid and paternalism, which will define the activity of the Church throughout the centuries, practically until the Second Vatican Council (1962–65). Society is not questioned by such assistance; social positions are respected, that of the rich and that of the poor; but a practice of aid to the poor by the rich will be developed. The activity is not dialectical, to the rich and to the poor. It goes from the rich to the poor, without taking into account the organizational and transformative ability of the poor themselves.[16] Thus, assistance is transformed into paternalism: the father that helps the younger and defenseless child. Within this spirit, the Church organized an impressive network of hospitals, leprosariums, hostels, dispensaries, as no other historical culture before it was able to do. A tremendous gallery of saints and servants of God—from Saint Zoticus, called in the Eastern Church the "feeder of the poor," to John Bosco, Saint Jose Maria Cafaso, the Cotolengo, and recently Mother Teresa of Calcutta—is characterized by the disinterested service of the poor.[17]

The *cura pauperum* found its formulation in two basic principles that summarize the assistive attitude of the entire ancient Church: first, the individual is to be considered solely as the administrator of the goods at hand, never as their owner, because only God is owner; second, the surplus of the rich is what is needed by the poor, and as a result, alms are a necessity of justice and not an expression of charity.

The bishop, within the structure of Christianity, in spite of exercising power, was understood as the *defensor et procurator pau-*

perum, as we see exemplarily illustrated in the lives of Saint Basil, Saint John Chrysostom, or in such popes as Saint Gregory the Great and Innocent III.[18] The poor may appeal to the bishops to demand that the rich comply with their duty of charity and justice with the poor (the so-called *denuntiatio evangelica*).[19] Canon 59 of the *Statuta Ecclesiae antiqua* states that "the priests must refuse gifts from the oppressors of the poor."[20] The Council of Tours (567 A.D.) is rigorous in Canon 26: "Judges and the powerful who oppress the poor may be admonished by the bishop, and if they do not reform, they may be excommunicated."[21]

The time immediately prior to Saint Francis is particularly important in relation to the question of poverty. It is a time of weather storms, floods followed by droughts, destruction of crops, especially hard winters, and much hunger (from 1194 to 1205). Difficult situations tend to favor theological-pastoral reflection, as happens in similar circumstances, in a vigorous and courageous manner. There were discussions about the "rights of the poor." They came to affirm the thesis "unanimously accepted in the faculties of rights, laws, and theology, to know, that it is by divine and human right that the starving man forced to rob is innocent."[22] The basic law was formulated thusly: "By natural rights, all things are common, and in time of necessity all things must be placed in common."[23] The life of the poor is worth more than the property of the rich; in case of absolute necessity, the poor individual may spontaneously take what has been denied him or her. This implies a veritable moral revolution: from the economy of alms and gifts, proper to the ruling society, one moves to an economy of restitution by right. And the poor are recognized as having value in their own right. The poor cease to be seen as a piece of the vast machinery of history and salvation, poverty as a way to salvation, through patience, for the one benefiting, and of redemption, through generosity, for the benefactor. The poor are considered *vicarius Christi:* the individual makes real the presence of Christ as judge, demanding the practice of charity and justice with the naked, the hungry, the jailed, etc. Furthermore, the poor individual is "judge and porter of heaven," acting as intercessor before the Eternal Judge. Finally, the poor prolong the incarnation of Jesus, suffering servant within history.[24] Service to the poor implies a service to Christ himself. There was yet a more radical demand: not only to give alms, share

things, but also to give oneself and become poor through love for
the poor and for the poor Christ (*paupers Christi*).

Essentially, the twelfth and thirteenth centuries, as we shall see
in more detail, are characterized by the great religious movements
based on the evangelic and apostolic life, in imitation of the crucified and poor Christ and in the radical living of poverty. They are
the Patareni, the Poor Men of Lyons, the Waldensians, the Albigensians, the Humiliati, and others, all of whom took the part of the
poor, especially in the cities, giving rise to the most radical movement in all of the spiritual history of Christianism.[25] The Franciscan mendicants, Servites, and Dominicans are expressions of this
more general movement. By means of all of them, the step was
taken from *liberalitas erga pauperes* (generosity with the poor) to
conversatio inter pauperes (living together with the poor). They are
the precursors and founders of the modern preferential option by
the Church for the poor and oppressed.

With the advent of modern states, the charitable institution was
not only reserved to the Church. Princes and kings themselves assumed the responsibility for attending the poor. They favored the
communities of lay people to help the marginated; they instituted
dining rooms for the poor, pension funds; and they promoted the
reform of hospitals and the creation of a policing of the poor with
the aim of identifying the working poor (poor artisans) and the
vagabonds, sending them to prison, into forced labor, and even to
the gallows.

With the industrial revolution and the breakdown of the medieval order, the problem of the poor took on a gravity it had not had
before. One only needs to read the pages of *Das Kapital* by Marx
about the historical origin of capital and the social cost demanded
of the poor, submitted to every type of pressure and exploited by
rising capitalism, soulless and fierce.[26] With the acceleration of the
production process within the forms of capitalism, the problem of
the poor became worse on a worldwide level. The Church felt overcome in its ability to help. Tied to a conception of a society of
order and a perspective of corporations, it arrived too late at a
comprehension of a society of classes. The social encyclicals, mon-
uments of ethical sensibility, do not go beyond calling for exterior
changes, remaining far from the Marxist contribution to the development and organization of the libertarian struggles of the work-

ing class. The condemnations remained at the level of the abuses of economic systems; only in 1967, with the *Populorum Progressio* of Paul VI, does it risk classifying capitalism as a "fatal system" (no. 26).[27]

In summary:

> It is moving to verify the enormous effort of the Church in resolving the problem of the poor. But what escaped her is what we see today: that all of that affective and effective generosity left for the poor only the crumb of the social process. The economic machine and the social system functioned for the benefit of the closed groups, the dominant groups, among whom was the ecclesiastical hierarchy itself. The Middle Ages did not see, nor could it see, that poverty was a structural problem. It was tied to the idea of society as a static system; one could change social levels, but not the number of levels, the social system. Because of this, the history of the Church until the end of the Middle Ages (and we would say until very recent times) is the history of the poor Lazarus and the good rich man.[28]

The project of the base is not to make of Lazarus a guest at the table of the rich, but rather that in their situation they may earn their food. Because the Church failed in this, it ceased being a Church for the poor without becoming a Church with the poor, much less of the poor.

A Church with the Poor

In the measure to which a majority of Christians and the hierarchy itself go deeper into the realm of the poor, what is pointed out is the urgency of another form of more effective presence among the poor. This penetration in the land of the poor allowed the Church to discover the passion of the poor, the institutionalized violence to which they were submitted. The much-exalted development had taken place behind them and even against them, such that the abyss between them had widened further, in global terms. It discovered primarily the value of the poor, their ability to resist, the dignity of their struggle, their solidarity, their strength, associated with the gentleness for life and family, their ability to evangelize the entire Church. In the midst of them, the Church was slowly changing its vision: instead of seeing the poor from the perspective of the rich, it began to see them with the eyes of the poor.

From the very social place of the poor one can perceive the necessity for structural changes in society in the direction of a greater justice, communion, and participation.[29]

At Medellin (1968) and with greater consciousness and radicalness at Puebla (1979), the Latin American Church has made a clear option of preference and solidarity for the poor;[30] this choice is according to Pope John Paul II, a Christian option of the whole Church.[31] The Church wants to be at the side of the poor, to restrengthen its transforming potential, to incorporate itself in their process of liberation.

Because of this, option is here the same thing as conversion of the Church, as is expressly stated in the final document of Puebla (no. 1140). It implies a displacement of social position, from that of the elite to that of the poor.[32] This is the novelty of this option as opposed to other forms of presence by the Church among the poor. With its solidary option, the Church overcomes the merely moralistic and assistive vision and assumes a political perspective. It no longer wants to be only present in the institutions of aid; this assistive attitude does not take into account the very strength of the poor. Now they have their organizations and their struggles. The Church proposes to support their cause and be with them in their hopes for change. From the poor, the whole social system is questioned and a more humanitarian and symmetrical alternative is postulated. The Church, starting with its own internal wealth, will organize itself in a more popular and participatory way; it will permit the emergence of base Christian communities, in which the poor and Christian people express their faith and live the Gospel in a way committed to social change in the direction of the goods of the Kingdom, which are a more authentic fraternity and a more effective participation. The Church is incarnated more and more in the world of the poor, and it tries to reach them with poor means. It would like to be a Church with the poor.

This option is not exclusive, but rather preferential (Puebla, nos. 1134, 1165). The Church does not deny its essential universality, but defines the place from which it would like to begin to realize that catholicity, that is, from the poor, and afterward, the others. It begins with those who were also the chosen ones of the historical Jesus (Lk 4:17–21), and extends to others without distinction.

The option for the poor is an option against their poverty, being that it is an evil that God does not desire, because it is the fruit of impoverishing and exploitative mechanisms (nos. 30, 1160). To accept poverty in solidarity with the poor implies opting for social justice, committing oneself to the poor in the integral liberation of all for a more just and fraternal society (nos. 1136, 1154). There are already martyrs of this option in Latin America, who seal with their blood the new pact of the Church with the oppressed.[33] Nothing is more symbolic than the gesture of Pope John Paul II, on his visit to Brazil, upon giving his ring as supreme pastor to the *favelados* of Vidigal (Rio de Janeiro).

This question of the poor, so essential to the Gospel itself, is being converted more and more into the *punctus stantis et cadentis* for the whole Church. It becomes credible to the degree that it makes its own the causes of the poor, which are universal causes: justice for all, participation for all, respect for the human rights of all. Assuming such universal causes, the Church itself concretizes and builds up its universality. The destiny of Christian faith itself is played out in the destiny of the poor, a faith that finds its reason for existence and verifies its truth as it is lived out as the integral liberation of humanity, and especially of the poor.

FOR THE POOR AGAINST POVERTY: A SEMANTIC EXPLANATION

This quick glance at the diverse attitudes of the Church in relation to the poor reveals to us various faces of poverty, which constitute a profoundly ambiguous reality. Many are the poor, by different titles, and in diverse forms. On the one hand, poverty is presented as an evil that should be eliminated; on the other, as a virtue. Which poverty are we talking about? An effort at explanation is necessary to reduce the ambiguities to a minimum. And the most adequate method is the dialectic: for each case it must be clear what the opposite of poverty is. Thus, the relative nature of poverty appears, that is, a reality that cannot be analyzed in itself, but rather in contrast to another. Each new meaning carries a distinct value judgment and demands a certain attitude on the part of the Christian. As we will have occasion to prove, poverty, on the one hand, appears as a manifestation of sin, while, on the other hand, it may be one of the highest expressions of love and solidarity. Poverty is cured with poverty, freely accepted as identification with the poor and as a denouncement of their iniquitous situation.[34]

Poverty: An Evil—The Lack of Means

As we have already pointed out, this meaning is the most direct and immediate; it signifies the penury of means and services destined to satisfy the basic needs of human life, including specifically human needs, whatever they may be, of participating in the cultural, social, and political process, as Puebla rightly ascertained.[35] Such poverty may not be culpable, because that which causes it may not be persons, but rather poor physical means, the technical backwardness of a whole human group or the cataclysms of nature. This poverty does not cease being an evil, because it impedes the expansion of life and cuts short human existence. It manifests itself as the submission to the harsh struggle for survival, limiting freedom from the higher activities of the human spirit, such as intellectual, moral, artistic creativity. In spite of this, the spirit is not drowned but only blocked; the culture of silence and poverty also have their dignity and give testimony in their own way to the thirst for transcendence of human subjectivity.

The opposite of this type of poverty is the wealth of means for the production and reproduction of life and society. To opt for the poor implies struggling against their poverty and a conscious and organized effort in the creation of technical and social development that allows for a growth of life beyond the struggle for survival. The Gospel spirit can be a factor in the integral human growth. Missionary history has made manifest that to evangelize means also to liberate. The Christian faith announces that the reign of God is begun here on earth, and must be built by people to the degree that they create material and social relationships that favor the growth of life. The idea of Kingdom is associated with a certain abundance and overcoming of the dread of poverty. In the last three decades, especially in the poor countries of the Third World, the Gospel has been profoundly used as a factor of growth and liberation,[36] as a form of anticipation and historical concretization of the Kingdom of God. In the definitive Kingdom there will be no poor or poverty, but rather the just and brothers in the shared wealth of God. Poverty, then, must be conquered, and has a negative relationship to the glory of the Resurrected One and to the destiny to which the world is called. In spite of this, we must observe that poverty-need, as well as wealth-abundance, contain a danger of dehumanization: the first because it directly threatens survival, and the second because it drowns life in luxury and excessive consumption. Because of this, the Christian utopia in which one refers to goods and services is not based on either poverty or wealth, but rather on the just measure, granting privilege to being over having, and on solidary uses over individualistic consumerism.

Poverty: A Sin of Injustice

There is a poverty produced by social relations of exploitation (Puebla, nos. 30, 1160). It has to do with impoverishment on the one hand and enrichment on the other, generators of true injustice, which is the sin that God despises. "Are not the rich those who oppress with pride?" asks the apostle James (Jas 2:6). In our situation, this impoverishment is a real social sin. The Old Testament is full of invectives against the rich, who with their tricks and demands engender the poor (cf. Is 10:1-2; Am 2:6-7; Mi 3:1-3; Hab 2:6-8).[37] This injustice challenges God Himself. The Messiah will be the liberator of the poor: "There will be justice for the lowly, he will save the needy and destroy the oppressor" (Ps 72:2-4). "You have unmade the slavery that oppressed the people, the oppression that afflicted them" (Is 9:4-5; 11:1ff.; 61:1-3). Jesus, revealing his messianic consciousness, appeals to this tradition as bearer of the good news for the poor, making them just and returning to them their usurped rights (cf. Lk 4:17-21). The poor are the chosen ones of God and of his Messiah, not because they are ready and adorned with moral virtues, but because they are poor. The reason is not in the poor ones, but in God, who wants to choose them (cf. Mt 11:3).[38] This is the meaning of the blessedness of the poor, according to Saint Luke (Lk 6:20): the concrete and historical poor, made poor and objects of exploitation, will be the first beneficiaries of the goods of the Kingdom, which are supported in justice, without which no good has a firm base.

The opposite of this type of poverty is justice. It is from here that to opt for the poor signifies, in this acceptance, to opt for social justice, for the necessary changes without which the productive mechanisms of justice and equity cannot be created, against the poverty-injustice and the social system based on the accumulation of goods in the hands of a few and in the exploitation of the work of the vast majority. It is not uncommon for this meaning to be the most frequent in the Gospel (fifty-three times), whereas only once does it speak of poverty or the poor in spirit (Mt 5:2).

Poverty: An Evangelical Way of Life—Total Availability

The Gospel, continuing the long-standing testamentary spirituality of the *anawim* (the poor and humble ones of Yahweh), postulates a spirit of total availability and trusting surrender to God and brothers and sisters. We receive everything from God, and as such, everything we receive comes to us; we are almsgivers before God; we are to keep nothing for ourselves, but rather, all that we have and are must be placed at the service and need of others and of the will of God. This Gospel spirit is indispensable in order to belong to the Kingdom; this is the anthropological project of Christians. To be poor is the same thing as being simple, detached, ready to give and receive.[39] This is the meaning of Matthew's version of the Beatitude of the poor (Mt 6:3). The opposite of this form of poverty is Pharisaism, bragging, arrogance, and self-promotion, so criticized by Jesus in his Gospel. To opt for the poor means, then, to opt for a radical conversion of the heart in the face of a culture of *hubris*, of self-affirmation, of autonomy at the side of the domination of others, support and exaltation of the strongest, most intelligent, and most powerful. Jesus lived this radical way of life to the point of surrendering his own life. To follow Jesus is to appropriate this ethic.

Poverty: A Virtue and Its Asceticism

All spiritual masters lived and preached a life of poverty as an ascetic way of liberating the spirit of the instinct to possess and the drive to enjoy material goods. This virtue is not specifically Christian. It is imposed as a demand for any spiritual ascent and any true creativity in any dimension of the human "poetic." Poverty as a virtue is situated somewhere between the scorn of goods and their affection. It deals with moderate and sober use of goods, which may vary in accordance with places and cultures, and whose meaning, however, is always retained: the freedom of spirit for the works of the spirit, which are freedom, generosity, prayer, cultural creativity. Poverty-asceticism signifies wisdom of life. The opposite of this form of poverty is prodigality and irresponsible waste. To make an option for poverty, within this understanding, translates into an ecological mentality, responsible for all the goods of nature and culture, for a sober and anticonsumeristic life, in the face of a society of production for production's sake and consumerism for consumerism's sake. Puebla said that "in the present world, this poverty is a challenge to materialism and opens the doors to alternative solutions to consumer society" (nos. 1152).

Poverty: Expression of Love for the Poor against Their Poverty

Anyone who is not poor may become so through solidarity, and more, through identification with the poor. One feels full of compassion and gentleness for the inhuman situation that afflicts the poor and decides, through love, to live together with them, participating in the hopes and bitterness. This solidarity is born of a sacred anger and expresses a protest: this poverty, which is impoverishing and dehumanizing, should not be; the poor are generally scorned and abandoned; almost no one is concerned for them, except God. They belong to the dimension of the heart, to the spirit of kindness, as we said before, the ability to attain, thusly, transdescendence. Only love can allow a realization in which the objective conditions for such realization are denied. If poverty-injustice results from a lack of compassion and solidarity, then it will be compassion and solidarity that will heal poverty-injustice.

This was the way of Jesus. He, who "was rich, became poor for us," with the aim of overcoming the differences between persons, some in affliction and others in consolation, so that there "might be equality" (cf. 2 Cor 8:9–13). He lived poorly, as all who live by their work, because he was a carpenter (Lk 6:3), and he was always poor, living from alms, as any itinerant preacher; he had a common purse with his disciples, and even came to the aid of other poor ones (cf. Jn 13:29). In his Passion and the cross he knew the extreme forms of poverty. He wanted to put his most decisive presence for salvation in those overlooked by the world (Mt 25:31–46).[40] A presence of identification takes human form in the poor ("You did it to me. . . . You did not do it for me"), a kind of prolongation of the Incarnation (through the special inclusion of the poor in the mystery of the Incarnation of the Word). He is present in the poor or rewarding those who enter into solidarity with them. He is also present in the poor as the sacrament of the historical poverty that he accepted as his way of entering into humanity. He could have been incarnated in an economically rich way, in a sacred and religiously privileged way (high priesthood), in a politically powerful way (imperial). But he did not do that, simply choosing the hard road of those who need to work to live as the poor live.

The opposite of this solidary poverty is selfishness and insensitivity, a sin that today reaches universal dimensions. In this sense, the option for the poor can be realized in two ways: living with the poor, participating in their struggle for survival, helping them with the profoundly humanizing lenitive of conviviality, even without the perspectives of exterior changes or organizing themselves, fighting for the cause of their liberation, searching for ways of overcoming poverty toward more just and participatory forms of work and social life. One or the other form expresses love and the desire to take part in the lives of those who have the least, but who are also called to be in communion and fraternity.

THE RADICAL OPTION OF THE POVERELLO FOR THE POOREST

After these semantic clarifications, we are better prepared to understand the depth of the radical option of Francis, father and brother of the poor, for the poorest of his day. As in all historical happenings, the primitive Franciscan movement sinks its roots in the material, ideological, and religious conditions of its time. As is seen from much study, the twelfth and thirteenth centuries were swept by numerous religious movements that intended to live the *vita apostolica et evangelica* with great radicalness. The great contemporary Franciscan historian Cajetan Esser states: "Each one felt deeply called and obligated to imitate in his personal life the life of Jesus, that is, to orient his life in conformity with the Gospel of Jesus. Life according to the Gospel is the new ideal of the Christian adults at the height of the Middle Ages. This ideal is the irreplaceable criterion for determining whether or not a Christian life is authentic. All adopted a form of life according to the Gospel, also called *vita apostolica*."[41] Those who spread this ideal were most of all the itinerant preachers, for the most part lay people, who translated bits of the Gospel into the local language and who preached in the towns and cities, especially in the squares, where the representatives of the feudal system met in their decadence, together with the merchants and artisans, integral to the growing system. They lived in extreme poverty, because they were determined to imitate the way of life of the primitive apostolic community and that of Jesus Christ himself.

The Waldensian movement was particularly impressive. Peter Waldo, a rich businessman from Lyons, got rid of all his possessions in 1170, distributed them among the poor, made a Provençal translation of biblical texts, and began to preach among the people, especially among the textile workers. He went to Rome, and with difficulty, gained the approval of Pope Alexander III and the Second Lateran Council (1179) for his poor life style, although he was prohibited from preaching to the people if not solicited by some priest (*nisi rogantibus sacerdotibus*).[42] These new religious lived by the work of their hands or from alms as they went, two by two, from town to town and from city to city. Many members of this movement contributed to the renewal of religious life; others became radical and opposed the clerical Church, falling into heresy; and some were incorporated into the new mendicant orders: Franciscans, Dominicans, and Servites.

Francis, son of a rich merchant who traded in textiles with the south of France, where the religious movement achieved greatest meaning, heard without doubt talk of Waldo and of the other religious leaders. Some insist that the priest of the little chapel of the Portiuncula, who accepted the recently converted Francis, was a Waldensian.[43] Not without reason, the most important student of these movement, H. Grundmann, could write: "Francis and his first companions come from exactly the same mold as Waldo. Thus, in Franciscanism, from its beginnings, are represented those social strata that are considered everywhere as bearers of the pauperist movements: rich bourgeoisie, nobles, and priests."[44] Essentially, the first companions of Saint Francis came from the upper classes, although the movement was open to all without discrimination.[45]

An understanding of the history that grants importance to the social infrastructure in the rise of movements and charismatic leaders points up the similarities between Francis and the ideals of his generation. But there is also something peculiar to Francis. He is not as interested in the following of the apostles or in the return to the primitive life of the Church in the way of common goods and the spirit of the Acts of the Apostles as in following, imitating, reproducing, and representing the life of Christ; against those who opposed the hierarchical Church he also underscored the *secundum formam sanctae Romanae Ecclesiae*.[46] But with reference to poverty, nevertheless, he continues the living of the ideals of previous generations.

Option for the Poor: Change in Social Class

In terms of social extraction, Francis belonged to the rich bourgeois class that was part of the Italian communes, which were in the midst of the already perceptible crisis of the feudal system. His father, Pietro Bernardone, was a very prosperous businessman (*praedives*, says Celano), linked to the marketplaces in France, to the greatest cloth merchants of the day. The first biographies portray the young Francis completely immersed in that world of the rich. He lived as the "bohemian minstrel,"[47] becoming the leader of a society of libertine youth, devoted to the Provençal *cantilenae amatoriae*, to the minstrels' songs, wandering through the streets singing the exploits of Charlemagne, of King Arthur and the Knights of the Round Table, in a romantic atmosphere of the humanities, of golden youth, with jousts and sumptuous banquets.[48] As an older youth he took his father's place,[49] "living in an atmosphere marked by the greed of the businessmen" and "dedicated to the lucrative deals of commerce."[50]

During an illness, he entered a crisis and "began to think of himself in a different manner"; and "nothing satisfied him" anymore.[51] Afterward, he began to give hints of "a notable affection and extraordinary generosity and compassion for the poor."[52] The biographical sources show that the more the crisis grew (including his sporadic attempts to become a knight), the more there grew in him "mercy for those who had nothing."[53] Taking advantage of the absence of his greedy father, he filled the table with loaves of bread with the intention of giving them to the poor.[54] On one occasion, everything he received from a sale in a market in Foligno, including a horse, he gave to a poor priest at the chapel of San Damiano so that it might be used "to help the poor and for the rebuilding of the little chapel."[55] He began to live, then, for the poor. He had not changed his social status; he remained within it, and once in a while took part in the parties of his young friends.

His vocational crisis deepened, and he "distanced himself little by little from the life of business,"[56] until there was a break with his father in front of the bishop. His father demanded the money obtained from the sale of some cloth, and Francis stripped himself of his clothing, and completely naked, took refuge in the arms of the bishop.[57] From that moment, "he began to live *with* the lepers";[58] he cured their purulent wounds, gave them alms, and treated them with great tenderness.[59] It was one more step. He began to abandon his own world and enter the world of others. It was something more than solidarity for the poor; it was a search for identification with them, a living with the poor. For three years he lived like a hermit, dressed in the habit of a hermit, tied with a leather thong, carrying a staff, wearing sandals.[60]

On one occasion, in the little church of the Portiuncula, he heard the Gospel of the day,[61] which told of how the Lord sent his disciples out to preach (Mt 10:7–10; Mk 6:89; Lk 9:1–6), without silver or gold, without money, without purse, without bread, without a staff for the road, without sandals, and without spare clothing. Francis understood that message as directly addressed to him, and he said, "This is what I want, this is what I have been looking for and what I want to practice with all of my heart."[62] It was his true conversion. He took off his hermit's habit, threw away the staff, and dressed himself in only one tunic, which he tied with a cord. He decided to live among the lepers and the poor.

At this point, he still does not live for the poor, nor with the poor, but rather like them, helping them with alms, and later with work. "The father of the poor, the little poor Francis, identified with all the poor, did not feel good seeing someone poorer than he; it was not because of vanity, but because of a feeling of true compassion. And if it is true that he was content with an extremely miserable and threadbare tunic, he many times wanted to divide it with another poor man."[63] Thus does his first biographer describe the "de-class-ification" of Francis.

With great simplicity, he writes toward the end of his life in his *Testament:* "The Lord led me, brother Francis, to begin to do penance in this way; because, as I was in sin, it seemed to me a very bitter thing to see a leper. And the Lord Himself led me among them, and I practiced mercy among them. And, leaving them, what had seemed bitter to me, became sweetness of body and soul; and after this, I stayed a short time before leaving the world" (*et postea parum steti et exivi de saeculo*). Here is clearly shown the privilege of the poor in the conversion process of Francis. Compassion for the crucified ones led him to immerse himself in the compassion of the Crucified.[64] The Crucified, in turn, helped him deepen his vision of the crucified ones.

The text of 2 Corinthians 8:9 has a tremendous meaning for Francis. It illumines his biographical itinerary, similar to that of Christ: "Our Lord Jesus Christ, in his goodness, being rich became poor for our sake, that we may be made rich through his poverty." Christ himself changed his condition (Phil 2:6–8), just as Francis changed social position.

This change of social position is expressly indicated by Francis as "leaving the world" (*exire de saeculo*). World does not here have a physical-cosmological or moral meaning,[65] but rather social. World, then, means the group of conditionings and relationships that constitute a concrete society. Francis essentially abandoned his social class, the dominant order of his day; he left the society of the *maiores*, as they were called, and decisively wanted to be *minor;* he also abandoned the type of Church strongly organized in its pyramidal hierarchization to become *frater*, brother to all, without any hierarchical title.

He left one place and defined another with which he identified himself: *feci misericordiam cum illis*, he had mercy on them. He considered the lepers in particular as the great sacrament of Christ. He tenderly called them "my Christian brothers" or "my brothers in Christ."[66] From them, he organized all understanding of his life, of God, of Christ, of the meaning of fraternity.

In the famous chapter 9 of his *Regula non-bullata*, he says to his brothers that "they should feel satisfied to be among the common and rejected people, the poor and the weak, the sick, the lepers, and the beggars of the street." And so the primitive Franciscan community worked and lived in the leprosariums, completely identified with the poor. When Francis, in his letters or admonitions, is presented as *homo vilis et caducus, vester parvulus servus,* putrid and fetid, miserable and vile,[67] he is truly describing his physical condition. According to the testimonies of the time, he dressed in a mended and dirty tunic, and his appearance was insignificant, because he was short and ugly, and he spoke with great enthusiasm without worrying about the rules of grammar and rhetoric.[68] As can be seen, he was someone not very different, in appearance, from many of the hippies of recent times.

It is interesting to note that at the very moment that the bourgeoisie began to be born as a social class of businessmen with a capitalist mentality, which would engender such injustices and impoverishment, there was also born its dialectical negation with the conversion of Saint Francis, which was a conversion to the poor and the poor Christ. This conversion was affective, because it implied overcoming the natural repugnance that misery provokes, until it is transformed into "sweetness of body and soul," as he says in his *Testament*. It was also an effective conversion, as much as it accepted the social position of the other; from the solidarity of the good bourgeois he went to the identification of the rich man who becomes truly poor with the poor and like the poor. Let us take a look at how Francis arrived at this foundational experience.

Radical "Disappropriation" and Total Rejection of "Appropriation"

To be able to be identified with the real poor and with the poor Christ, Francis does not want to own anything, and he simply asks his followers to "observe the holy Gospel of our Lord Jesus Christ, living in obedience, without property and in chastity."[69] His ideal is to live *in paupertate altissima et mendicatione humilima*,[70] and he achieves it in a way that still startles us. Francis asks a total "disappropriation" of all forms of possession, material, spiritual, and religious goods.

First, the disappropriation of *material* goods: the brothers should dress like the poor, that is, with a simple tunic, mending it when necessary.[71] Nothing should be considered theirs: not houses, not churches, not convents.[72] Later, with the evolution of the pastoral ministry of the order and the assimilation of the brothers as a support to the priests, it was permitted that they accept churches and convents, but on the condition that they consider themselves "pilgrims and strangers in this world."[73] He begs the brothers not to ask Rome for any type of privilege, but rather that they be at the service of all; if they are not permitted to preach in some place, they should go to some other. They should work with their hands, and if they do not receive a salary commensurate to the work done, they should not demand it, but rather have recourse at the table of the Lord, begging alms. They should never receive money. Francis knows that money is a true fetish, "a demon and poisonous serpent," in his words.[74] In case of manifest necessity they can receive alms "like other poor people." He does not accept anyone into his company who has not given all of his goods to the poor and who has not become radically poor himself.[75]

Francis wants to live a poverty that leaves him in total insecurity, like those who have no kind of economic resources even for the following day's subsistence. He reduces possession to the minimum: clothing, instruments of prayer (breviary), instruments of work,[76] and sacred objects.

Human beings do not only possess material goods; they possess *spiritual* goods, science, and natural talents, functions that imply honorability, hard-earned virtues. These are the most enduring and precious goods, because they are personal. Francis realizes, precisely, that in this area there may develop the spirit of appropriation, which distances us from communion with the poor and with the poor Christ. Thus, to the learned who want to follow him, he asks that they renounce their knowledge to "be totally nakedly embraced by the Crucified."[77] No one is to appropriate the ministry of preaching,[78] or the office of superior, whose name should not exist in the fraternity because the guardian is like a mother and like a servant who washes the feet of the rest.[79]

Those who, though poor themselves, scorn "those who wear delicate and colored clothing and eat and drink things of high quality" sin against highest poverty.[80] They "treasure," and for the same reason sin against, poverty who are irritated by the sin of others,[81] and are like the Pharisees who do not repent of their own sins. Although one may be jealous and tolerant, one is not poor if one shows oneself to be unable to tolerate any criticism, becoming irritated and bothered.[82] True poverty is always accompanied by humility that supports and accepts everything, because the *I* stripped itself of all desire for self-affirmation, justification, and imposition. For this reason, in his praise of the virtues, Francis prays thusly:

"O holy lady poverty, may the Lord keep you with your sister holy humility."[83] True poverty is demonstrated by obedience, which demands the denial of the most precious gift of God: will and freedom. Obedience does not demand so much to do the will of another, always within ethical imperatives, but rather to give oneself to the other for love.

Finally, there is a subtle form of ownership, which makes fraternity impossible: not being interiorly happy at the virtues of others, their efforts on the way of Perfection and the certainties of their fidelity to God. Francis is aware of this type of appropriation, which implies "hiding the money of his Lord" (cf. Mt 15:18),[84] not giving credit to the true author of all, God. In the *Regula non-bullata* he makes a vehement call to the brothers: "In the charity that is God, I beg all my brothers, preachers, contemplatives, workers, clerics as well as laity, to be humble in everything, not glorying or finding joy in themselves, nor internally exalting themselves for their words or good deeds, nor even for any good that God does, says, or works in them and for them."[85] An individual cannot own anything that only belongs to God. Not even the certainty of one's own salvation is ours, but rather solely God's. In spite of all our efforts at rising "we will only be saved by His mercy."[86] Our own future is in the hands of God, and we should not try to assure it.

With the strength of this radicalness, Francis makes illegitimate any appropriation (*appropiatio*), soul of our capitalist system, in the following way: ownership looks for security, prejudices the community and neighbors, is inspired by passion and pleasure, wounds the soul, searches for one's own well-being, degrades work, overvalues the corporal, sees in intelligence and will a private property, is the road of sin and the devil, enemy of all good, taking sides against God and denying his Kingdom. Furthermore, it appears to be the desire for wealth, domination, envy, presumption, pride, hunger for honor, and glory, and it promotes intrigue.[87] On the other hand, disappropriation is rejection of security, the worries of this world, money; it is liberation for others, liberation of wanting to know, being right and dominating; it is to be small; it serves the Kngdom of God and conversion and is the best way of following Christ. Disappropriation is seen in poverty, in humility, joy, service, obedience, simplicity, and purity of heart, love.[88]

To Be Radically Poor to Be Fully Human

An endeavor as radical as this needs heroic virtues because it demands peaceful living with misery, hunger, suffering; living at the mercy of intemperate weather and every class of privation. A chronicler of the time, Buoncompagni, recounts that the brothers "put up with horrible and inhuman torments."[89] But they did not suffer them poorly, as if laden with a heavy burden from which they could not be freed. They lived with a joviality, joy of living, enthusiasm, and courtesy that left everyone puzzled.[90] What is the mysticism that sustained and enlightened these hardships of poverty? What is Francis's secret?

The spiritual savvy that gave life to Francis's radicalness with regard to poverty was in the impulse of Eros that searched for identification with the poorest and with the poor Christ. Poverty is never for Francis an end in itself or a purely ascetical path to be followed. It is the means to an incomparable good: union and fraternity with the forgotten and with the suffering servant, Jesus Christ.

Francis had intuited, as we said in the previous chapter, that fraternity between persons and the encounter with God are blocked and even destroyed by the desire for possession. We place between ourselves and others the things that we selfishly possess, as well as interests. We are afraid of exposing ourselves, heart to heart; we prefer property that gives us security but that separates us from others as well as from the roots that feed our humanity: gentleness, conviviality, solidarity, compassion, and love. Francis's endeavor is *in plano subsistere*,[91] that is, to live on the plain where everyone meets and "con-*frater*-nizes." Poverty is the effort at removing any type of appropriations, so that the encounter beteeen persons may result, making fraternity possible. To be radically poor to be fully human—this is the endeavor of Francis in relation to poverty. Only the *vere expropiatus*, the one who has truly disappropriated him, can become a *frater menor*, a brother of all.[92] This orientation of poverty to fraternity is clearly expressed in his *Testament* of April–May 1226, wherein he says: "I briefly state my desire to my brothers in three words:[93] . . . as a sign of remembrance of my blessing and testament, always love one another; . . . love always our Lady Holy Poverty and keep her; . . . always live faithful and submissive to prelates and clerics of Holy Mother Church." First of all in his intent is fraternity, radical poverty, and the way to achieve it.

Poverty is also a path for identification with Jesus, who lived among us. We have already referred to the gentle compassion of Francis toward the mystery of the humility of God Incarnate. Naked, he wanted to follow the naked Christ,[94] who "was not ashamed and was poor and a guest and lived by alms as much as the Blessed Virgin and his disciples."[95] Many times, speaking of poverty and the following of Jesus, he cited Matthew 8:20: "Foxes have lairs and the birds of the sky their nests, but the son of man has nowhere to lay his head."[96] This was already enough to possess nothing, to not be less than Christ himself.

The real poor and the poor Christ are the criteria of true poverty. Francis never speaks abstractly about poverty. He calls it, in the courtly language of the knight, Lady Poverty; if he establishes a *sacrum commercium*, he does not do so in the sense of hypostasis or substantivization of Poverty for poverty; he speaks in this way of all the virtues, in his particular style, imbued with Eros and Pathos. He is not lost in speculations about *quantum*, how much can be possessed without violating poverty. When, disgracefully, the order was split later by quarrels concerning levels of poverty, if one could or could not own this or that thing without ceasing to observe the poverty that we all promise to observe, it gave a clear indication that poverty was no longer thought of in terms of the real poor, but rather as a way-of-being had been transformed into an ascetical and moral virtue, one more added to the list.

Francis always confronts his poverty with these two objective realities: the real poor and the poor Christ. If he finds a poor man poorer than himself, he takes off his own clothes in order to be on his level and serve him. The Franciscan sources are full of gestures, compiled in a series by the *Mirror of Perfection*[97] and by the second biography of Celano. Even the only copy of the New Testament, used for the meditation of the brothers, is given to a poor woman, with this comment: "The New Testament itself commands us to help the poor. I believe that God values more our giving alms than our reading."[98] If it means helping the poor, it is worth stripping the altar of the Virgin. When he set norms for the clothing of the brothers, for the building of houses, and other such things, he took as a reference the poor and not some abstract determination, always saying *sicut alii pauperes,* "like other poor people," or "in the way of the most simple."[99]

Humanization through Fraternity

Life, within the parameters of strict poverty, was burdensome and hard. Francis and his companions seemed *quasi silvestres homines,* half savages, as it says in the *Legend of the Three Companions;* others thought of them as essentially "insane, because their life was like those who have no hope, because they hardly eat, walk barefoot, and are covered with the most vile clothing."[101] We ask ourselves: How, beyond the mysticism of gentle and compassionate identification with the poor and the Crucified, did they make sense of their want? No one lives by mysticism alone. Life has demands that cannot be opposed permanently. How did they humanize this objective dehumanization that is poverty? It is precisely within a context of poverty that Francis places the problem of fraternity. Each one's poverty implies for others a challenge, in order, to their care, gentleness, and the creation of an atmosphere of openness and security, denied by radical poverty. For Francis, *having* has been toppled from its pretension of granting security and humanization to persons. Only care for one another truly humanizes life, as Heidegger also showed in his *Being and Time.*[102] Care is the way of being human.

Francis says in the definitive rule: "And wherever the brothers are or find themselves, may they be cordial with each other. And in confidence let each one make known their needs, because if a mother loves and cares for her child of flesh, how much more should one love and care for his spiritual brother?"[103] The brothers should be *domesticos invicem inter se,* they should act as members of the same family, as true brothers. This spirit rebuilds the home abandoned for love of the poor and the poor Christ, and gives back emotional security, though there are no material goods. But, in case of necessity, they can eat "all the dishes that are placed before them," because "necessity knows no law."[104] Francis is for poverty, but he is much more for life, with the sensibility that it demands.

The same sensibility is revealed in relation to the sick: "The other brothers ought to serve them as they would like to be served themselves."[105] For those who live absolutely unprotected, community, in fact, is everything. In spite of his idealization, Celano tells us of the life of this fraternity, which was poor but joyful and full of humanity: "They desired to meet, and together they were happy; on the other hand, absence was painful for them, separation was bitter, and parting sorrowful."[106]

The detachment of poverty grew into a great liberation of love and the disinterested enjoyment of all things. The only one who can taste the world, without denaturalizing its reality, is the one who renounces the spirit of possessing it. Only then does it cease to be threatening and is introduced into the arena of human fraternity. As Jacopone da Todi, the great Franciscan poet of the thirteenth century, sang:

> *Povertá é nulla habere*
> *e nulla cosa poi volere*
> *e omne cosa possidere*
> *en spirito de libertade*

THE CHALLENGE OF SAINT FRANCIS

The encounter with Francis always causes an anthropological commotion, because it leads us to confront ourselves with the most demanding, the highest, and the most radical. In this sense, he is an incomparable saint, as the great historian Joseph Lortz called him,[107] or as others have called him, the first after the Only Son (Jesus Christ). Of the meanings of poverty that we have defined above, he lived, above all, poverty as an evangelical way of being of total availability and poverty as an expression of love for the poor against their poverty. Total availability was expressed as *minority:* to always be the last and to be as far below as possible in order to be able to serve everyone, without disputing the position or power of anyone. This does not at all mean masochism, but rather the highest form of relationship, which engenders liberty in the other; Francis and his "little poor people" lived this spirit of minority with courtesy and unassumingly, with joy and without false pity. Francis also lived this attitude before God, before whom he felt like "a miserable little worm, your most humble servant."

The radicalness with which he lived the identification with the poor does not cease to amaze us. Only love for the disinherited of this world could keep him faithful without wavering. In them, he met the poor Christ. Humanitarian love was transformed into Christian love; anthropology became theology and christology.

As we will see in the next chapter, identification with the poor did not lead Francis to organize the poor with the aim of overcoming their real poverty. You can't squeeze blood out of a turnip. The possible consciousness of his time did not place the question in political and social terms, as we do today, and so we must do so in obedience to our consciousness.

However, Francis achieved an incommensurable liberation of the poor. What makes poverty inhuman is not only that it impedes the satisfaction of basic needs. It is scorn, rejection, exclusion from human life together, the permanent brainwashing of a negative and unqualified image of the poor, developed by nonpoor classes. The poor end by thinking of themselves as abject and despised. No one is on their side; the good luck of life and of others is against them.

The liberation achieved by Francis consisted in being a rich young man, the flower of the bourgeois society of Assisi, who took on the condition of the poor and lived like a poor man. He served the poor, touched them, kissed them, sat at the same table with them,[108] felt their skin, lived in physical communion with them. These contacts humanize misery; they give back to the poor the sense of their human dignity, never lost but negated by the society of the healthy. Francis created a fraternity of brothers open to the world of the poor; he saw that it was the will of God that he remain in the world, and not retreat to hermitages or convents.[109] These attitudes of Francis imply a protest and an act of love—a *protest* against a society that expels the poor from its midst and hides them in inhuman places outside the mainstream of life. So Francis's movement is the center of the periphery; the chapels he rebuilt and the places in which the first brothers lived were on the outskirts of the city of Assisi: San Damiano, Rivo Torto, Le Carceri. But it is, above all, an *act of love*, because he was not interested in the poor while remaining in his father's store, but rather became one with them to the point of identifying with their situation, living with them.

Francis has left us with a serious question: is it possible, as he tried to do, for any group to live the Gospel utopia of radical poverty as a way of achieving a real fraternity?

We know that he and the primitive Franciscan community lived this Gospel adventure in a heroic and almost delirious way. They

were filled with sufficient amount of mystic, human, and Gospel
Eros in order to face the unmoving historical forces against them.
But we also know that the entire history of Franciscanism, starting
with the last years of Saint Francis's life,[110] moved in another direction. More and more, poverty as identification with the poor
and living by pure necessity were abandoned and became a conception of poverty as an ascetic and mystical identification with
the poverty of the incarnate God who, being God, became human,
and not a human god who voluntarily became poor.[111]

This does not signify a betrayal of the founder; nor ill will or
mediocrity. It is a domestication by the imperative of history.[112]
From the moment that the personal charisma of Francis was
changed into a movement, there arose, by strong necessity, *nolens-
volens*, the need for organization, with its inevitable logic, which
is the sensibility of rationality and the meaning of viability at the
service of the weakest. So Francis had to accept, without understanding why, the necessity of rules, novitiates, houses of formation, more to avoid abuses than to maintain the charism. The
movement grew into a religious order that surpasses all other religious orders. Being an order approved by the Holy See, it saw
itself obligated to define its place within the global dynamic of the
Church of the day. It was a work of the fine religious sense of Popes
Gregory IX and Honorius III to have respected to the utmost the
original intentions of Francis. But, notwithstanding, the order had
to bow to the demands of the structuring of the Church's endeavors, which had been growing since Gregory VII (1073–85) and
whose roots are found in the changes of Constantine in the fourth
century. The Church, as we have already pointed out, was a Church
under the regimen of Christianity. And this means that it occupied
a place of political, economic, and religious ruling power in the
feudal system. Whoever holds power is condemned to exercise it
with the logic of all power, which establishes a basic and primary
division between those who have power and those who don't.

The poor are by definition those without power (*impotens*); they
are placed, as a consequence, at the margin of the system of power.
A Church under the regimen of Christianity will never be able to
be the Church of the poor; structurally it acts as a Church for the
poor, if it is faithful to its evangelical dimension. Franciscanism,
which in its original conception was presented to the world as liv-

ing of the Gospel from the poor and with the poor, through the process of domestication that is inevitable within the Church, suffered a violent transformation: it was forced to be spiritualized and to translate its practices of solidarity with the poor, within the world of the poor, into practices of solidarity with the poor from the position of the rich. Franciscanism never forgot its sources, the poor; but its presence among them will have to be from the sociohistorical position of the Church, which is a position of power. It relates to the poor through power; and instead of maintaining relationships of identification, as Saint Francis did, it will maintain relationships of assistance and paternalism.

Today there are different historical and theological conditions. The Church is no longer sought after by the powers of this world to codirect the paths of human destiny. We have inherited a Church that strongly feels it must make a preferential and solidary option for the poor. The Church can be, today, essentially what it wants to be: a Church of the poor and from the poor, of all who are open to the message of the Gospel. Puebla consecrated this choice of value for the entire universal church.

Puebla, with its option for the poor, signifies a formidable challenge for the Franciscan spirit. In the first place, it makes us uncover the original meaning of Francis's option for the poor, with the poor, and like the poor. Second, it challenges us to look critically at the real forms of the living of poverty in the Franciscan movement within the context of the inheritance of cooptation by the Church under the regimen of Christianity. Puebla says: "It is important that we reevaluate, in community, our communion and participation with the poor, the humble, the lowly. It will be, at the same time, necessary to listen to them, to accept their deepest aspirations, to value, discern, encourage, correct, with the desire that the Lord guide us to make real our unity with them in one body and one spirit. This demands of us . . . the personal and emotional renunciation, according to the Gospel, of our privileges, ways of thinking, ideologies, preferential relationships, and material goods" (nos. 974–975).

As one can see, this deals with an invitation to the conversion to the foundational charism of Francis. If at some time the Franciscan spirit was inexorably coopted by the civilizing endeavors of the feudal Church, it is imperative today for Franciscans to let themselves gain through the new spirit of the Church, that is, in Gospel terms, much stronger and clearer than the spirit of power.[113] It is important to live Franciscan poverty once again as solidarity and commitment with the poor. In the next chapter, this demand will be dealt with in greater detail.

Independent of the way the Franciscans resolve their own fidelity to the charism of the Poverello within the context of a changed Church and a changed society, Francis's living of poverty constitutes a great anthropological and social challenge. It is not uncommon to admit that highly participatory social forms are only possible on the condition that there first be built an infrastructure capable of producing abundance. In terms of the present-day problem: concrete democratic socialism (as distinct from that achieved in the East) would only be viable on the presupposition that capitalism had accomplished its historical mission; this would be in making possible an enabling and encouragement of the entire process of production with the aim of creating goods that would be socialized for everyone, on economic, political, and cultural levels. The construction of socialism would only be real upon the foundation of a society of abundance. On the other hand, socialism, as history has shown, degenerates into totalitarianism of the state, with its bureaucracy, political parties, and army, making the collective participation of the people impossible.

What was extraordinary about the teaching of Francis was his intent to live in complete fraternity under the presupposition of a poverty voluntarily accepted in order to be at the side of the poor, and with them, to build all human relationships, always beginning with those who have least, with concern for those who are least. The poor are seen as an apparition of divinity. This perspective, traditional within Christianism, never reached a social and cultural form; it remained confined to religious meditation and charity inspired by that meditation. In some tribes in Africa, the handicapped are considered the permanent presence of the divine, and they are all adopted like children, being considered fathers and mothers; society integrates, humanizes, and saves them as human persons, contrary to our societies, which normally reject the poor and handicapped.

Francis's endeavor seems concretely possible on the level of the individual and small groups. That is because it presupposes an ethical, humanitarian, and mystical desire, impossible to demand of a larger group. Francis was conscious of the uniqueness of his experience; he calls himself *pazzus*, crazy.[114] This expression is very common in the biographical literature of the day.[115] But it is important to make clear what things made him think of himself as "crazy." Not the Gospel, nor the ideals of Jesus' preaching of radical fraternity with all persons, but rather the good sense of history that favors viability in the game of conflicting interests. According to historical sensibility, fraternity alone is possible on the foundation of abundance. Francis is above this type of reasoning. Inflamed by Eros and Pathos, he tries to realize fraternity where there are not the objective and sensible conditions, amid the poor and with the poor. Another type of sensibility goes with this "insanity": the sensibility of utopia, reasoning proper to the hope principle, the logic of infinite desire.

This courage on the part of Francis for the impossible, lived with such seriousness, but without any fanaticism or resentment, is the reason for the fascination he holds for us. Beyond the tragedy that comes so often throughout history, there remains the challenge of the great spirits like that of Francis, who dared to believe in utopias. Was his teaching worth it? The most important poet of the Portuguese language, Fernando Pessoa, forms the answer for us:

> *Is it worth it?*
> *It is always worth it*
> *for to the soul, nothing is small.*

Liberation through Goodness

THE CONTRIBUTION OF SAINT FRANCIS TO THE INTEGRAL LIBERATION OF THE OPPRESSED

One day, the blessed Francis, near the Church of Saint Mary of the Angels, called to Brother Leo and said to him: "Brother Leo, write this down."

Leo answered: "I am ready."

"Write down, what perfect joy is," Francis continued.

"A messenger from Paris arrives and says that all of the teachers at the university want to enter the order. Write: that is not perfect joy. And though all of the prelates beyond the Alps, archbishops and bishops, and even the very kings of England and France were to enter the order, write: that is not perfect joy. And if you were to receive news that all our brothers went to preach to the infidels and converted them all to the faith, or that I received so much grace from God that I cure the sick and do many miracles: I assure you that that is not perfect joy."

"What, then, is perfect joy?" asked Brother Leo.

"Imagine," Francis continued, "that I return to Perugia on the darkest of nights, a night so cold that everything is covered with snow, and icicles form in the folds of my habit, hitting my legs and making them bleed. Shrouded in snow and shivering with cold, I arrive at the door of the friary, and after calling out for a long time, the brother porter gets up and asks: 'Who is it?' And I respond: 'It is I, Brother Francis.' The porter says: 'Be on your way. Now is not the time to arrive at a friary. I will not open the door for you.' I insist and he answers: 'Be on your way right now. You are stupid and an idiot. We are already many here and we do not need you.' I insist once more: 'For the love of God, let me in, just for tonight.' And he answers: 'Not even to talk. Go to the leper colony that is nearby.'

"Well, Brother Leo, if after all this, I do not lose patience and remain calm, believe me, that is perfect joy, true virtue, and the salvation of my soul."

The radical poverty lived by Francis in solidarity with the poor and in following of the poor Christ gives us the opportunity to reflect on the characteristics of liberation that arise from that attitude, and on the contributions of his practice to the global process of the emancipation of the oppressed of our day. Christian reflection during the last decade developed what we call the theology of liberation, which implies a vigorous articulation of the discourse of faith with the discourse of society, on the level of Christian effectiveness in terms of the liberation of the poor who, in the Latin American continent, represent the vast majority of the people, both Christian and oppressed.[1]

The theme of liberation is not new, though it certainly is the strongest impulse in modern culture. Generally, we can state that the history of the past five centuries centers in large part on the process of emancipation. The first significant emergence came with Galileo Galilei and the liberation of *reason* from within the religious totality that impeded the free flight of thought in the discovery of the working mechanisms of the world. Then, there was the liberation of the *citizen* from the absolutism of the kings, to see the citizen as the real bearer and delegate of political powers, as Rousseau thought. With his writings, there was the liberation of *spirit* alienated in physical matter by way of the transfiguration of absolute Spirit. With Marx, attention turned to the liberation of the *proletariat* from capitalist economic domination with the aim of arriving at a socialist society without class distinctions. With Nietzsche, there was the liberation of *life*, shortened and suffocated by the sophistication of metaphysics, morals, and culture. Freud developed a whole plan for the liberation of the *psyche* from its interior bonds (neurosis, psychosis, etc.). Marcuse launched the manifesto of the liberation of *industrial man*, reduced to only one dimension by assembly-line production. The worldwide feminist movement promotes the liberation of *women*, faced with a patriarchal and male culture, toward a less sexist and more personalistic society.[2]

All modern revolutions promoted and promote the widening of the sphere of human liberation: the scientific revolution, the bourgeois revolution, the socialist revolution, the atomic revolution, and the cybernetic revolution.

We can see that this whole emancipatory process is done behind the Church's back, beside it, or against it. The contribution of Christian-Catholics was minimal. However, the Judeo-Christian influence is not absent from all these movements. Some of the distinguished representatives of modern liberation were Jews: Marx, Nietzsche, Jung, Marcuse, Einstein. They carried with them the liberating wisdom of the Old Testament prophets and the sense that history continually should be made to be worthy of the Creator.

THEOLOGY OF LIBERATION: THE FAITHFUL GRANT LIBERATING POWER TO THE FAITH

Liberation theology is understood in the thread of these great movements of emancipation that characterize the modern age. It was born on the periphery of the world and the Church, in Latin America, and is spreading to Africa and Asia, where the poor see in it the articulated voice of their poverty, which demands liberation. It may be the only time, in the last few centuries, that faith has proposed to be a concrete factor in the liberation of the oppressed in a conscious and planned way.

At the base of this theology of the poor there is a spiritual experience of protest and love. Above all, it is a holy ire, the very virtue of the prophets, against the collective misery of the poor. With the words of Paul VI in *Evangelii Nuntiandi*, taken up by the bishops of Puebla: "want, chronic and endemic illnesses, illiteracy, poverty, injustices in international relations and especially in commercial interchanges, situations of economic and cultural neocolonialism sometimes as cruel as former political colonialism" (nos. 30, 26). This reality does not please God, because it humiliates His children. It needs to be changed. Second, underlying the theology of liberation is a committed love that translates into the preferential and solidary option for the poor. This option, as we analyzed in the previous chapter, implies, in the first place, a change of social position that includes, at the same time, an epistemic conversion: to try to see reality and history from the point of view of the anguish and hopes of the poor.[3] From these, it becomes patent that society must change and that, just as we are living, we find ourselves in a situation of social and structural sin. Second, the transformation of society must be made by the poor and their own real strength; they are the new emerging historical subjects. For this change toward a more human and more just society for all (not only for the oppressed of today), the basic component is Christian faith itself, because the vast majority of them are Christian and poor. The Gospel and Christian faith have no reason to legitimate existing powers (which under analysis are revealed as oppressors) or to lull the lower and oppressed classes. On the contrary, by reason of its very origin and essence, the Gospel of Jesus Christ is a factor of concrete and historical liberation. Only through a perversion of the living of faith has its liberating ferment been castrated.

Fundamentally, liberation theology deals with two principal tasks: first, to point out the theological relevance of freedom movements. Historical liberation is never just historical. There is in it, objectively, grace or sin, independent of the interests of the actors or ideological signs that they inspire. In other words, salvation and the Kingdom of God are realized, objectively, within these processes, *nolens-volens,* because everything is open to and penetrated by the ultimate will of God. But the Kingdom is made present and is anticipated to the degree to which these processes are ethically defensible, that is, they signify the creation of true and better meaning.[4] This perspective allows the rereading of the liberation movements of the past centuries and of the secular culture resulting from them as theologically relevant, although they have not been supported by the Church, and although, in some cases (the socialist and workers' revolution), they have taken a position contrary to Christianism. Grace and the Kingdom do not find in the Church exclusive mediators, but rather privileged ones (on a sacramental order). Christian faith in the universal presence of God and Christ within history makes it possible to read with a theological key the emancipatory processes that produce humanization and a greater sphere of freedom. The Church is the place where this consciousness is developed, and also where it is realized in a conscious manner, as the celebration of salvation that is in the world and not only in the Church. Without this conscious explanation, historical liberation would be real, but not complete; it would be theological (it would always have to do with God), but it would not be sacramental (represented by an adequate discourse and celebrated as a community).

Second, the theology of liberation deals with emphasizing the liberating aspects that are present in the Gospel, in the life and praxis of Jesus, and in the great tradition of the Church. Faith is salvific only when it is translated into a praxis of love; today, this praxis rises above the merely personal and must assume a structural and social character. Salvation comes about not only in liberating movements, but also in every human expression; but today it finds its dominant and most valuable expression in the social and political dimension, because this is the area where the greatest human decisions are made and it is where God is primarily served or offended. The bishops in Puebla rightly stated: "Liberation is being realized in history, that of our peoples and our own personal liberation, and it reaches the distinct dimensions of life: the social, the political, economic, cultural, and the whole range of their relationships" (no. 483). Even more so, the Church "censures those who tend to reduce the sphere of faith to personal or family life to the exclusion of the professional, economic, social, or political spheres, as if sin, love, prayer, and forgiveness had no importance in them" (no. 515).

The big question that challenges Christians in every poor area is how to be true Christians, how to announce the joy of universal fraternity (because we are all children of the heavenly Father), in a world of wretches and exploited. We can only be so, in fact, if we live Christian faith in terms of human advancement and liberation. Faith, essentially, is not exhausted by these expressions; but it would not be a true faith, nor the faith of Christ and the apostles, if it did not include liberation from misery, meaning dehumanization and an offense to God Himself. It has to do with a liberating evangelization, urging a Christian practice that implies also a transformation of society, helping to form a new humanity within sociohistorical structures that result in greater fraternity. This, fundamentally, is what is proposed by liberation theology.

It is not enough, however, for faith to want the transformation of society. Effectiveness depends on the intelligent comprehension of social mechanisms, especially of those that generate poverty, and of the steps necessary for a qualitative change toward more human ways of life together. One must always keep in mind the specific contribution that faith can offer. It liberates, but not in any specific way, not losing its own identity. Furthermore, it never liberates alone; it offers a contribution to a process that has other faces, with other actors and interests. But it can and should, as an expression of its fidelity to God and humanity, offer its support to the liberation of the oppressed.

To aid in the effectiveness of faith, liberation theology develops a methodology, that is, a specific procedure of reflection and practice. First, it is important to see, analytically, the sociohistorical reality. In this way it is discovered that we are living in a society of classes with antagonistic interests. Objectively, the poor are poor because, the way society is organized, since they have the strength to work but not the capital, they are placed on the margin. This is what dictates, not only in economy but also in every social, political, and educational organization, imposing the values of those with capital. To gain their most basic rights, the workers have had to shed much blood. Pablo Neruda recounts the struggle of the workers in the desert areas of Chile, rich in potassium nitrate, in order to gain the minimum of health care, because many were dying in the mines.

> During one of those strikes, the company police carried away seven leaders. The guards rode horseback while the workers, tied to a rope, followed them on foot along back roads. They were assassinated. Their bodies remained tied beneath the sun and cold of the desert, until they were found and buried by their companions. . . . In 1906, in Iquique, the strikers went down to the city from all of the nitrate fields, to place their requests before the government. Thousands of men, exhausted from the journey, united to rest in a plaza, in front of a school. In the morning they were going to the governor to explain their petitions. But they were never able to do so. At dawn, a colonel and his troops surrounded the plaza. Without a word, they began to shoot, to kill. More than six thousand men fell in that massacre.[5]

Similar events are routine in societies dependent on and peripheral to capitalism. To be unfamiliar with the bloody struggle of classes carried out by the capitalists against the workers is to cruelly ignore the cries of millions of nameless and permanently held back workers. In this moment of seeing, poverty is defatalized and shows itself for what it is, as the bishops in Puebla said, "not a chance stage, but the product of definite economic, social, and political situations and structures" (no. 30), by which "the rich get richer at the same time that the poor get poorer" (no. 30). Analysis brings to light these mechanisms, which normally remain hidden from the naked eye or mere empirical vision.

This analytical decoding having been done, one must *judge* that contradictory reality in the light of faith. Here enter into play criteria of a theological and ethical order, by which is judged the character of sin or grace, of order or denial of the historical plan of God for a just and fraternal society, of this class society. Then faith develops its own understanding of persons and society, and in order to achieve this, organizes its involvement around the social.

More important than to see and to judge is to *act*, though this must be enlightened by seeing and judging. At the time of acting, the Church dissects and thematizes the aspects of liberation present in its particular practice, in liturgy, in catechesis, in theology, in pastoral activity. The Church acts in a specifically pedagogical way, unblocking consciousness, leading people to take on a commitment among their brothers and sisters, in obedience to the commandment of love in its social dimension, creating a mysticism of societal transformation as a way to concretize and anticipate here in the world the Kingdom of God, beginning in the present and culminating in eternity. From its own identity in faith, the Church organizes the people in Christian communities, those in which the lowly meet, meditate on the Word of God, and enlightened by that Word, discuss their problems and find ways of solution. These base communities have an immediate and direct religious value, but they also achieve social importance because they are places for the formation of social conscience, responsibility, and the desire for change.

More than this, communication with other social groups that are also involved in the structural change of society is sought. Because of this, a Church committed to a preferential and solidary option for the poor supports the movements that are born of the base—free unions, peoples' associations that are concerned about the defense of those without power, their culture, their rights. Also important is communication with other social classes that have opted for the people and their struggles. Without their cooperation, no liberation of the base would be lasting. The Latin American bishops and the papal magisterium itself[6] has become conscious that, within our present-day situation, distinct from that of other times, "the Church has the duty to announce the liberation of millions of human beings . . . the duty to help the rising of this liberation, to give witness to it, to see that it be total; none of this is foreign to evangelization" (Puebla, no. 26; *Evangelii Nuntiandi*, no. 30). This commitment, which not a few have condemned as an incitement to class struggle, meant defamations, persecutions, and even death for many pastoral ministers, from bishops to simple peasants. If the divine liberation of humanity cost the blood of the Son of God, will not the lives of many persons be the cost of the historical liberation of the oppressed? It is the price one must pay for all activity that struggles to liberate the captive. Freedom is never freely granted; it must be attained in an arduous process of liberation.

FRANCIS: LIBERATED, LIBERATING, AND FREE MAN

If we want to look at the liberating dimension of Francis we have to do so within the correct epistemological consciousness. Otherwise, because of the lack of adequate interpretive keys, one could arrive at totally mistaken conclusions, such as: "We do not find in Francis any social concern; he did not want to change anything, he did not challenge anyone, nor was he against anything."[7] One must place Francis within his time. In the medieval world, religion dominated everything; it organized all of society. Although it did not stop being the ultimate, economics is interpreted from theology and religion. It is what establishes the theoretical arena, and all other subjects are found within that arena, utilizing the very language of religion. There is no place for the autonomy of the social as such in the age of Saint Francis, within the forms we have specified above. Because of this, to look for social liberation in Saint Francis, within present-day schemes of society or liberation, means to fail to find any parallel. The theme of liberation must be sought in categories such as poverty, love, rule, authority, fraternity, money, obedience, Saracens, etc.

Furthermore, we know today that subjects always maintain an interrelation with social surroundings. One does not need to be conscious of this, but the subject himself is structured independently of wanting or not wanting this. We have discovered ourselves as possible consciousness. Every human being sinks his or her roots within a situation determined by space and time; the very destiny of each individual is realized within a context that is not perfectly defined; one which is open to the possible, but takes shape while on one's personal journey. A social actor does not live and think whatever he or she wants, but rather what is possible to that actor within concrete social coordinates. As a result, one must always be understood within a wider process, within the dialectic of society-individual, personal destiny–collective destiny.

With reference to the theme of liberation, it is necessary to take into account another methodological fact: the importance of point of view. For many, the theme of liberation is irrelevant, because they do not participate in the anguish and hopes of the world of the poor. They do not pace themselves in the perspective of those interested in liberation, those who are poor, and all who have opted for them. Francis made, without any doubt, an option for the poor. His presence among them, taking into account his possible consciousness, signifies an objective liberation. To understand Francis's contribution to liberation it is necessary to have first defined, above all, the interests and commitment for the poor. It should not be thought that this could prejudice the analysis; on the contrary, it opens up the arena for just such an analysis.

All human knowledge takes place from a point of view or social position, that is, the conscious taking of a position by the subject who knows. To know is always to interpret, and to interpret demands the utilization of codes or interpretive keys. This is the objective condition of all knowledge. To want to see everything, globally, without any presupposition, without selective criteria, without a determined point of view and interest, means to resign oneself to not seeing anything or to place everything on the same plane, as if everything had the same value; it means to deny criteria of priority, to close oneself off from the meaning of historical perspective, and finally, to block all desire to critique visualized events.[8] To know, then, means to become a participant, but with critical distance and a sense of limits, of one's own point of view, because every point of view is the view from a point.[9] With this epistemological focus, we want to treat Francis's contribution to the category of liberation, and eventually, to the reality of liberation as a whole.

Francis: Liberated Man

Francis, as a social individual, emerges at a particularly privileged, and at the same time critical, moment; it is a time of ruptures: something old begins to die, and something new begins to be born. The feudal means of production experiences a shake-up, because its rule is threatened by the emerging merchant means of production of the common bourgeoisie. With his style of life, Francis reflects the crisis of the times and gives to it his personal version of the possible ways.[10]

The feudal system is characterized by the servile means of production. There is the master, owner of the *feodum* or fief, and the servant who depends on him, working for the sustenance of the owner as well as his own. All social relationships are organized within the context of pacts, alliances, oaths, generating a system of mutual fidelities within a strictly hierarchical structure. Each one has his place, the *maior* and *minor*, and thus the pyramidal *ordo* is forged, stable, and immutable. God is invoked as the guarantor of that order. Dionysius the Pseudo-Areopagite, following the line of Saint Augustine, created the justifying ideology of the feudal system with his *De Sacra Hierarchia*. The earthly order corresponds to the celestial, and so a cosmic harmony is the result. The concrete symbol of this cultural unity is found in the monastic life; living on the earth and from the earth and the principle of development reside in the vow of obedience to the abbot and of the vassal to the monastery. The Christianism of the feudal court will be clearly agrarian.

In the age of Saint Francis the communes flourished; there arose from them a new social class: the bourgeoisie-supported commerce and professional corporations.[11] In Francis's day, however, this system of order did not yet prevail, but rather freedom of interchange and free association and production. Most people took refuge in the villages, next to the displaced of the rural areas, the knights without a war, and the decadent nobles. The servants who could reach the cities achieved freedom. Every type of marginated and rejected person, adventurer, and leper conglomerated in the cities. What counts, however, is not the ownership of land or noble title, but rather work, money, gold, business, material prosperity, which produce confidence in oneself. A fitting ideology was developed for this new society to grant it cohesion and organization: the worth of the individual, personal experience, the value of work and corporations—all of it new.[12] Courtly love reflected this liberty and broke through the rigidity of feudal stratification. It was more a world of lay people than of clergy. The Christianism that began to be lived is of a particularly urban character, supported by personal living, considered to be more important than the insertion into a hierarchical order of pure and simple acceptance of the tradition or doctrine of the theologians.[13]

With Innocent III, the hierarchical Church achieved the utopia already present with Gregory VII: the creation of a universal papacy, marked by the fullness of religious and civil power. The *sacerdotium* was above the *imperium*. The conquest of the holy places in the land of Jesus was considered to be a collective shame and humiliation. These same popes promoted holy wars, the Crusades, mobilizing ideologically all of Europe, appealing to a veneration of the humanity of the pilgrim and suffering Jesus.[14]

What can a Church immersed in power and preoccupied with maintaining dominion over the world say to this new Christianism, born of the villages and of merchant activity? Practically nothing. There is a vacuum of official leadership because until then the Christian religion was feudal and not bourgeois, rural and not urban. To attend to the needs of the time it would have been necessary to have an evangelization of the people that was based on the witness of poverty and that had Gospel roots, and not in the reiteration of common doctrine elaborated by imperial religious power. Only thus would a minimum of credibility be safeguarded and a fitting religious meaning be developed for the situation.[15]

It is in this context that the religious movements of the time immediately prior to Saint Francis must be understood—of the Waldensians, the Albigensians, the Catharists, the Poor Men of Lyons, the Humiliati, etc. The great majority of the members of these groups were lay people (at the margin of sacred power), arising from the lower classes, speaking the language of the people (not the official Latin), coming from the cities, and presenting an answer to the religious and social demands of the age. They articulated an incisive theme for the situation: to lead an evangelic and apostolic life would be translated by apostolic preaching and a life of poverty. Not only men, lay and cleric, but also many women set out to preach and to live the Gospel and apostolic life.[16] One must place the practice of Francis within this context. He is not an agent of the system of that time, social as well as religious. This is very well expressed in his *Testament* by the expression *exivi de saeculo* (I left the world); he did not abandon *the* world, but rather that world, that is, that type of relationship and interest. He did not do so by means of a theoretical strategy of consciousness, verbally formulating an alternative and putting a new model into practice. This is proper to our age and to our possible consciousness. In Saint Francis's day it would have been impossible. Notwithstanding the above, we ought to point out that he was a great revolutionary, not a mere reformer. The reformer continues to be an agent of the system, reproducing it by means of the correction of abuses and the introduction of reforms. In an analytical sense, revolutionary means a creative fantasy to plan and to live something not yet shown. Francis, revolutionary, began to walk his own path; he himself confesses in his *Testament:* "No one showed me what I should do." But what he does represents, on the one hand, a radical criticism of the dominant forces of the time, and on the other, a strong response to the demands of the situation.

Seen from the point of view of a system that defines what is possible and what is not, what is sensible and what is not, the path of Francis seems like foolishness. The Poverello has a clear understanding of this. He literally recognizes: "The Lord told me that he wanted me to be a new fool in the world."[17] But this "foolishness" is the basis for a new form of living together, opening up the possibility for a new world. And this is what the Fratello essentially started.

Faced with a feudal system centered on the "greaters," Francis becomes a "lesser" and wants his order to be called the "lesser brothers," subject to every human creature. Faced with the bourgeoisie, organized on the backbone of wealth, Francis proposes the idea of radical poverty and complete rejection of the use of money.

Faced with the Church of the time, the hegemony of the *sacerdotium*, Francis is a lay person; and even though he becomes a deacon later on, he is not tied to any of the benefits.

He is presented as a man liberated from the ties of the different systems. This consciousness is manifested in the dispute with his father, who went to the consuls of Assisi to force Francis to return the money that he had distributed among the poor. They asked him to appear before them. Francis answers: "By the grace of God I am free [*iam factum liberam*], and I am not obligated to obey the consuls, because I am a servant of the Most High God." The consul said to his father: "Seeing that your son is in the service of God, it is not up to us to judge him" (*de potestate nostra exivit*).[18] This way out from power is a form of liberation for Francis. In the very make-up of the initial group, this desire for liberation from the social relationships of the time is evident. Of the twenty brothers who make up that group, six come from the aristocracy, two are doctors at the University of Bologna, four are *boni viri* (persons trained in the law and eligible to be judges), one is a priest, one a lawyer and member of the cathedral court, three come from the lower classes, two are of unknown origin, and Francis himself belongs to the emerging merchant bourgeoisie.[19]

All make a radical option for the poor and for the poor Christ, renouncing beforehand the new society that is being born. Before having recourse to alms, they work in the leprosariums as domestic help, or in the fields. Even as mendicants they stick to what is strictly necessary. Francis said of himself: "I was never a robber of alms, receiving or using them only in what was demanded by necessity. I have always been content to receive less than what was offered me, so that other poor people may not be left needy; to act any other way would be sinful."[20] The group of lay penitents (the Third Order), under the inspiration of Francis, although remaining in the world, in some way also left the feudal system; they vowed not to carry arms of any kind and they refused to take any oath and thus enter into the feudal hierarchical order.[21] By means of successive bulls, Pope Honorius III (in 1221 and 1226) and Gregory IX (1227) defended the members of the Third Order against the persecutions of the mayors of many cities because they had left the feudal order.[22]

More important than being liberated from the social organization of the time was to be liberated for a new form of sociability. Francis founded a truly utopic fraternity,[23] rooted in the radical equality of all: "None of the brothers are to have power or dominion, and even less among themselves . . . , but rather he who wishes to be greater must be their minister and servant."[24] Whoever assumes a position of coordination ought to act as a mother; he revolutionizes the relationship of the subjects with their ministers: the subjects may speak "as masters to their servants, because that is the way it should be, that the ministers be the servants of all the brothers."[25] He relates to his brothers as Knights of the Round Table[26] to represent the equality among everyone. Obedience is inscribed within the same spirit of fraternity: "The brothers ought to help one another spiritually."[27] In the rifts and failures of the community, the medicine is always in the spirit of fraternity: "So not worry or fret about the sin or bad example of others"; "admonishing him, instructing him and correcting him humbly and diligently"; "working with him as best befits them according to God."[28]

This fraternity opens outwardly. When they go out into the world, the brothers are to behave evangelically, living poorly, proclaiming peace, eating what is placed before them, avoiding any form of violence, giving whatever is asked of them.[29]

Leaving the world (*exire de saeculo*), as can be seen, implies a more profound entering into a new world. The most explicit form of this is "to go among the Saracens and other infidels" (*ire ad sarracenos et alios infideles*). The meaning of mission for Francis is not, above all, to convert the infidels and to expand Christianity, but rather to live the Gospel of universal fraternity "by submitting to all men through the Lord and professing that they are Christians." Because of all this, the living of fraternity and service beyond differences of religion and culture is closer to the truth of the Gospel than its mere doctrinal substance. Only afterward, "when they see what pleases the Lord, may they proclaim the Word of God."[30] Thus, the criterion is not ecclesiastical, reinforcing the Christian system, but rather theological, "to please God." This perspective of nonviolence toward the Saracens would be in contrast to the norm of violence of the Crusades of the age.

The fraternity would not be completely open and liberated if it were not open upwardly, in a true cosmic democracy with all creatures. To be truly fraternal, one must live fraternally with the birds, fire, water, the lark, the wolf, the worm on the road, treating all with respect and devotion, gentleness and compassion. In other words, the relationship with nature is not primarily one of ownership, but rather of living together and of conviviality. We all belong mutually to one another in a relationship of equality and symmetry. If there is some privilege with respect to the universality of goods, it must be a privilege for the poor, the defenseless, and the weak.

In relationship with the poor, Francis has a liberating vision, avoiding assistiveness as a form of presence among them. He did not point out to his followers any specific apostolic activity. He did not build hospitals, leper colonies, or other assistance works because he did not see the poor primarily as objects of aid. To be poor like the poor is superseded by being with the poor in deep solidarity. Francis voluntarily becomes poor to be able to live together with the poor and to form a community of life with them. Frequently one of the two brothers who went out to preach the Gospel was a leper. We see here, in action, not a pedagogy for the oppressed, but a pedagogy of the oppressed:[31] it is a way of rescuing the value of the poor, their power of evangelization, and of avoiding help that is not at the service of their creativity and values.

We have already referred to profound liberation in terms of humanization, which means a physical solidarity with the poor. Sharing their miseries, showing them affection, embracing and kissing them, consoling and helping them in their necessities—all this grants to poverty an imperceptible human dignity for those who need sensitivity; in other words, humanity denied to the poor and forsaken is not annulled, but rather is present there in contradictory signs; once these signs are accepted, they stand out as a spotlight and clearly illuminate humanity with its thirst for participation, respect, communication, solidarity, and its drive to rise above, beyond the struggle for pure survival, in the direction of the capture of what is beautiful, just, and sacred. And then one can appreciate the truth of Archbishop Helder Camara, the great realizer of Saint Francis in our midst: "No one is so poor that they cannot give, nor so rich that they cannot receive." In the giving and the receiving one is nourished and builds human life as human, beyond class differences. In the giving and receiving, the poor feel that their own poverty is humanized. In this context, courtesy, "sister of charity and one of God's qualities,"[32] availability, humble service, and the profound gentleness and compassion of Francis with the most needy all acquire relevance. They are forms of communication that humanize and liberate.

Francis, Liberating Man

One of the global values lived by Francis, together with poverty and minority, is peace. He does not go naively through the world; he knows that it is the *regio dissimilitudinis*[33] and that behind the dissimilarities are camouflaged injustices and violence. Especially property maintains strict ties with violence or the loss of inner peace and tranquillity. Bishop Guido judged it opportune to advise Francis about the hardness of his life because of the denial of any kind of goods. Francis responded, realistically: "Lord, if we had goods, we would need arms to defend them. And from there arise arguments and contentions that in many ways impede the love of God and neighbor. Because of this we do not want to have anything of our own in this world."[34] Every time Francis begins his preaching, he invokes peace, saying: "The Lord give you peace."[35] The greeting the brothers carry through the world is "Peace and all good." The whole order carries out a true mission of peace (*legatio pacis*).[36] Francis demands of the brothers a strict attitude of peace, to the point of recommending to them: "To everyone who approaches, be they friend or enemy, robber or highwayman, receive them with kindness."[37] In a society as turbulent as that of Francis's time, in which the robbers and highwaymen pillaged one city after another, this attitude could not seem less audacious and revolutionary. Even more: "The peace that is proclaimed in word ought always to be present in the heart. Let no one be provoked by us to anger or scandal, but rather let all, through your gentleness, be led to peace, tranquillity, and agreement. You have been called to this."[38]

What is asked, then, is that the brothers be actors of liberation from the ruptures and hatred among people. Francis himself took this mission of mediator very seriously, that is, he committed himself through peace as an authentic liberator, in Perugia, Bologna, Arezzo, and Assisi. In Perugia he asked that the knights who were training for combat with a neighboring city "be kinder with their neighbors,"[39] but in vain. In Bologna he worked toward the arrival at a new peace treaty,[40] overcoming the hatred that had divided the citizens. With Brother Sylvester he managed to pacify the city of Arezzo, "devastated by internal struggle."[41] In Sienna, after an ardent and persuasive exhortation, he pacified a group of citizens who were warring with and killing each other.[42] The reconciliation between the bishop and the mayor of Assisi is well known. The bishop had excommunicated the mayor, and he, in turn, had prohibited the buying or selling of anything to the bishop. Francis saw what was happening and, troubled, said: "It is a great shame for us, servants of the Lord, that the bishop and the mayor hate each other in this way, without anyone bothering to pacify them." Already deathly ill, he added a stanza alluding to this situation to the "Canticle of the Creatures": "Blessed may you be, my Lord, for those who pardon for love of you and who put up with injustices and tribulation. Blessed are those who persevere in peace because they will be crowned by you, Lord."[43] He sent two of his brothers to the mayor's palace, inviting him to the bishop's palace. And he sent the rest of the brothers to the bishop's palace, that they might sing the canticle with the added stanza. The mayor and the bishop met while the brothers intoned the canticle, and they were reconciled, "embracing with great friendliness and love."[44]

No less famous is the mediation of Francis before Sultan Melek-al-kamil, on the occasion of the Crusade.[45] In June of 1219 he joined the Crusades in Damieta; he saw the reigning violence and tried to stop the continuation of the war, without success, seeing the total massacre of the Christians.[46] But his efforts to achieve peace were worth the trouble. Suddenly, "without any defense," he was face to face with the Muslim army and was led before the sultan. The event is wrapped in legend, but Francis had a profound impact on the sultan, owing to his sympathy, tolerance, respect, and love for peace. The freedom of the brothers to be able to come and go and the custody of the sacred places of Palestine are linked to this peace-making gesture of nonviolence initiated by the Fratello.

With respect to the heretical groups, also poor and evangelic like Francis, but in conflict with the institutionality of the powerful, warlike, and rich Church, the Poverello acted with utmost respect and discretion. These heretics abounded in Assisi, Spoleto, and other neighboring cities, and even infiltrated the Franciscan movement.

In the saint's writings they are alluded to in an indirect way, as a protection against them; he never attacks them openly, because he does not want to destroy possible bridges by confronting them with arms, as was the policy of the times.[47]

He lives this same peaceful and creative attitude with the animals. He frees the caged birds, the sheep led to the slaughterer, and is indignant with those who mistreat animals.

The Liberating Strategy of Francis

What is the strategy utilized by Francis to liberate individuals from the feelings and practices that lead them to hatred and violence? Here we touch upon what is perhaps the most original point of his perspective in view of social and historical conflicts. We will deal with the subject by referring to two legends that, like all legends, preserve the spirit better than the letter of the events: that of the thieves of Burgo San Sepulcro,[48] and that of the wolf of Gubbio.[49]

In the first, a pedagogy of conquest and liberation is dealt with. The thieves were hiding in the surrounding forests and assaulting travelers. Driven by hunger, they asked for bread at the hermitage of the brothers. Moved by their need, the brothers helped them, although not without reservations: "Would it not be right to give alms to these robbers who have done so much evil?" They presented the problem to Francis, who suggested various steps to deal with the situation: a) carry their best bread and wine to the forest and shout: "Brother thieves, come here. We are your brothers, and we have brought you good wine." The thieves come and take the bread and wine served by the brothers. b) Only afterward will they speak to the thieves of God. But they will not ask them to abandon their life of robbery; it would be asking too much, without gaining anything. They will ask them instead to do what they truly can do: when they rob, not to hit or harm anyone. c) The following day, the brothers will repeat the same ritual, but with better provisions, such as bread, eggs, and cheese. d) The thieves will eat, and a new proposal will be offered them: to abandon that life of suffering and hunger; God gives those who serve Him all that is necessary for the body and for the salvation of the soul. e) Finally, the thieves will be converted because of the cordiality and kindness of the brothers and some of them will ask to join the fraternity.

As one can see, there is an explicit denial of accusation, censure, and condemnation. Francis's strategy gives way to goodness, cordiality, patience, confidence in the healing energies that are hidden in each individual, that may be activated through care and understanding. This perspective presupposes the overcoming of all Pharisaism and Manicheism, which place all good on one side and all evil on the other. It presupposes that in each person there is a possible thief and in each thief there is a possible brother. And the holy and good brother who is within each thief may be rescued if we treat him with gentleness, understanding, and care. It is the strategy of Francis—liberation through kindness.

This structure emerges with greater clarity in the legend of the wolf of Gubbio. Beyond its historical content, there is in this legend an analogous situation.[50] If we look closely, there is not an evil wolf on the one hand and good people on the other. What happens, in truth, is the use of the wild wolf, "great big, terrible, and ferocious," as the legend paints him, and of the other wolf of the city, armed and fearful. In other words, the legend deals with two actors who confront one another and whose only relationship is one of violence and mutual destruction. What is Francis's strategy? His perspective is not to force a truce, a type of balance of strengths inspired by fear. Nor is his strategy one of taking sides. He knows how to avoid Pharisaism, easily detectable in situations of conflict in which each social agent thinks more or less in the following manner: the evil ones are the others, not I, and so they must be destroyed. People don't question their own position for fear of discovering the evil wolf within themselves, living together in tension with the good. Francis's path is evangelical, a new path that is only discovered when each one is open to changing direction, directing themselves toward the other. The liberating challenge is to make new persons from the two types of wolves. This is how Francis perceives the poor-impotent and unarmed. He takes the path of the wolf. He does not go as a representative of the citizens; he goes as a poor man, as a citizen of the Kingdom of Heaven, fascinated by the newness of the Gospel. He closes the jaws of the wolf with the language of fraternity: "Brother Wolf, come here." He makes the wolf recognize his situation of "deserving the gallows, thief and murderer." But he also knows that "all of these acts were done out of hunger." With the promise of receiving the needed food, the wolf pledges not to harm anyone anymore. Francis has converted the wolf into Brother Wolf, a new being.

Francis's strategy with the wolves of the city (the armed and fearful citizens) follows the same path. He does not give them reason, but calls them to conversion: "Return to God, dearest ones, and do worthy acts of penance for your sins, and God will free you from the wolf of the present time and from the fire of hell in the time to come."

From this change in others may come peace: the wolf of the forest frequents the houses of men and they give him what is needed to live. And this peace is not the victory of one side over the other, but is the overcoming of sides and parties. It is true peace, which means, in a joyful expression of Paul VI, the "balance of movement." This movement is not oriented against the other but rather within and ahead: *within* through the conversion of each person, *ahead* through the creation of a convergence that is not a third way, but rather the new path of fraternity and peace, which no one possesses for themselves, but which all are invited to build.

Again, Francis's own procedure does not consist of exacerbating contradictions or denying the shadow dimensions of existence there where hatred, shame, and the spirit of domination reside. He gives a vote of confidence to the liberating capacity of kindness, gentleness, patience, understanding. "Francis understands the situations. Where we see nothing but vice and evil, he discovers a secret bitterness, a depth of ignored kindness, finally, a creature to save. That is, he is truly a good man."[51]

To achieve peace without any violence, he starts with his own person, as we have seen through many examples: the persuasive power of his word, poetry, and song. Peace is not only a goal that must be reached, but also a method. Because of this, the first biographies rightly emphasize that he always proclaimed the "Gospel of peace,"[52] that he was an "angel of peace,"[53] always beginning his preaching with the greeting "The Lord give you peace,"[54] and that he admonished the brothers, saying: "Go and preach peace to all."[55] This peace, Celano says, he proclaimed sincerely to men and women whom he met or who came to him. By this, he frequently found with the grace of God that the enemies of peace . . . became children of peace."[56]

Francis: Free Man

From the preceding reflections there clearly emerges the dimension of Francis's liberty. He was fundamentally a free man. The freshness of liberty shines through his gestures and words. This freedom is the fruit of the painful process of liberation. And the achievement of liberty reveals the maturity of a personality that always sought to rise above and be immersed in his own inner depths. Celano sees already in his very name—Francis—the expression "of a frank and noble heart; those who had the opportunity to experience his magnanimity know how generous and free he always was with everyone, and with what strength and vigor he despised the things of the world."[57] All of these qualities created the practice of an immense freedom, the primary source of our fascination with Francis.

The very rule of the "lesser brothers" expresses the sovereignty of liberty; a minimum of law and a maximum of spirituality is found in it, a minimum of organization with a maximum of Gospel.[58] When later some brothers, "noted for their knowledge and doctrine," suggested to Cardinal Hugolino the necessity of some rules and prescriptions to facilitate the organization of the community, Francis, angry, took the cardinal by the hand, led him before the assembly of the brothers, and defended freedom with these words: "My brothers, my brothers, the Lord showed me the path of humility and simplicity. Do not speak to me of another rule, not that of Saint Augustine, nor that of Saint Benedict, nor that of Saint Bernard. The Lord told me that He wanted to make of me a new fool in the world, and He did not want us to follow any other path of simplicity and the way of humility constitute the course of liberty because they imply a process of simplification, that is, a liberation from the superfluous and extra elements and a contraction of the essential.[60] For Francis, the essential is Christ, and Christ is found in the Gospel, which he wanted to follow like children who imitate their elders with simplicity, in the way that each one understands this. The Gospel life is understood by Francis as a "passing through the world" as a pilgrim and stranger, without any stability. When Lady Poverty asked the brothers where they lived, they led her to a mountain. With a gesture, they showed her the extent of the horizon and said to her: "Lady, this is our cloister."[61]

Because the world is wide, there is a place for everyone, and for the path of each one in the following of the Gospel. In Francis one can see a deep respect for each individual, because each one is led by the Spirit of the Lord. The rules (*bullata* and *non-bullata*) are full of expressions that invite freedom, creativity, and respect for the personal decisions: "as seems best to you and to God";[62] "What the Lord inspires you"; "do so with God's blessing"; or "in conformity with the Gospel"; "as seems best to you." For example, when he deals with entrance into the order, the candidates "sell what they possess and force themselves to distribute it among the poor; but if they cannot do so, their goodwill is enough. And the brothers and their ministers must be careful in asking for temporal things, so that they, as the Lord inspires them, dispose of these things freely."[63] Thus, he leaves to the free decision of each one the mending of the habits or not, to have the books necessary for liturgical prayer or not, to have tools for work or not, the liberty of eating what is put before them, the freedom to choose work that is not contrary to the simplicity of Franciscan life, the liberty to associate or disassociate the work from the sustenance of life, the liberty to remain among Christians or to go among infidels, the freedom to choose the way of being present among them, by means of service or preaching, and many others.[64]

Nor is it strange that, in light of this lived freedom, Francis would want the Holy Spirit to be the minister general of the order,[65] because "they ought to desire, above all, the Spirit of the Lord and its holy operation,"[66] and they must always obey the Spirit. If, on the one hand, Francis is radical in his option for poverty and simplicity, on the other he is profoundly free with himself and with others. He dresses extremely poorly and eats what the others leave him, but he remains free of all envy or interior Pharisaism. Because of this, he exhorts the brothers "not to scorn or judge those who wear colored and fancy clothes, who eat and drink fine foods, but rather that each one judge and scorn himself."[67] In this way, he admonishes them not to think ill of the rich in spite of the profound ambiguity of all wealth. In this way, he is free to frequent the houses of the powerful of this world, that "they offer and even impose upon him their hospitality," as he himself says;[68] but not even in this way, to the scandal of Cardinal Hugolino, does he accept to eat with them, going out to beg alms[69] and making it clear that his basic option is for poverty; he is present among the rich, but from the poor.

Francis gives the reasons for this liberty among others and also among the rich, considered as lords and brothers, "because they are brothers inasmuch as they are creatures of God and they are lords inasmuch as they help good people to do penance, granting what is necessary to the body."[70] As will be pointed out, Francis places himself in a dimension of depth, from which the differences between individuals are second or third, notwithstanding their truth or weight. There is an umbilical cord between persons that cannot be cut, due to the fact of being permanently tied to God and in the hands of the Father of goodness. To understand this is to live free of all ruptures produced by history and the desire for power, to experience the unity of all beyond divisions, which are always painful. Even more, Francis is free to such an extent that he tries to live cheerfully with all contradictions. To the minister of the "lesser brothers" who complains of the animosity and even violence of which he is the victim, Francis responds: love those who treat you this way, and do not even demand that they be better Christians; and if they ask for mercy, no matter how numerous their sins have been, treat them with mercy; and if they do not ask for it, ask them if they do not want it. And if they sin over and over again, love them more than you do me, and have compassion with these brothers.[71]

Again, what determines relationship is goodness and not the spirit of vengeance. One does not honor the Creator by cursing his creatures. Francis does not want to speak overly much of human miseries, in order that, with our reason, we do not come to be unjust with God.[72]

The highest expression of the freedom of Francis is contained in the parable of perfect and true joy. Although the most extraordinary things may happen to a person, although one may be turned away from one's own house, "if [one] has patience and remains calm, this is true joy, true virtue, and the soul's salvation."[73] True liberty is realized when an individual has decided to live with all creatures, independent of their situation, serving them courteously, even the animals, as Francis wanted.[74]

Because of the freedom that he achieved for himself, Saint Francis encourages all the true processes of liberation that search, by means of solidary action, to create and to widen the arena of liberty.

·4

Creation of a Popular and Poor Church

THE CONTRIBUTION OF SAINT FRANCIS TO A CHURCH OF THE BASE

It is the year 1216, in Perugia. Lugubrious Gregorian chants rise from the cathedral. The solemn *Planctum super Innocentium* is being sung. Pope Innocent III has died after eighteen years of a glorious pontificate. With him the Church has achieved the *dominium mundi;* the priesthood finally has conquered the empire. The pope had become the sovereign of all the kings and princes. Honor, glory, power, pomp and brilliance, the triumph and wealth—all light the torches of the fisherman's boat.

Nothing stops death, who is lord of all vanity. The pope's skiff lies before the high altar. He is covered in furs, jewels, gold, silver, and every symbol of the double power, sacred and secular. Cardinals and princes, monks and the faithful pass before the catafalque. It is midnight. The pope is alone in the darkness. Some thieves come into the cathedral and in a short time strip the body of all its precious vestments, the gold, the silver, and the insignias. And the body is left naked, already almost decayed. In fact, it is verified, that is, what he himself had written so crudely while still a cardinal "about the misery of the human condition" comes true.

Legend has it that a little poor man, miserable and ill-smelling, has hidden in the dark corner of the cathedral to watch, to pray, and to spend the night. He takes off his worn and dirty tunic, a tunic of penance that his friend Pope Innocent III had authorized him to wear in 1209, when he came before him with his companions, and he covers the naked body of the pope with it. This is the destiny of the wealth of this world, and it is the salvation of evangelical poverty. The former impoverishes, the latter redeems.

The future cardinal, Jacobo de Vitry, holy and wise, says: "I went into the church, and I could see in utter faith how brief is the glory of this world."

The little poor man whom all call, tenderly, the Poverello neither said or thought; he only did: he made himself naked to cover the nakedness of his friend. Francis of Assisi, the saint.

The Second Vatican Council (1962–65) signified, primarily, a collective effort at the codification of Christian faith in response to the demands of modern humanity; this is its great theological value. At the same time, it defined, officially, what the Church was, the realm of Christianity, with a specific type of Christian presence within society; this is the cultural significance of the council. The realm of Christianity, as we explained previously, is characterized by the alliance between sacred power, embodied in the hierarchy, and civil power, concentrated in the state and the ruling classes.[1] The Christian message is made present among the people through the mediation of the ecclesial institutions in conversation with the institution of the state or controlled by the dominant sectors of society. Within this model, the Church is structured around the pole of sacred power, linked with civil power.

FROM A CHURCH OF THE CLERGY TO A CHURCH OF ALL THE PEOPLE OF GOD

Beginning in the fourth century, with the Constantinian conversion, the entire Church (community of the faithful with its hierarchy) is invited to accept the political and cultural advancement of the West. To the degree to which the Church involved itself in this task, it became more and more necessary to have a body of specialists that, with cohesion and coherence, could carry on this historical challenge imposed by the injunctions of the times. This body of experts was made up of the clergy. In the interest of historical efficacy and acting in the face of other events (with the fall of the Roman Empire, the Church was the only universal body), power was gradually concentrated in the hands of the clergy, civil as well as religious power. Beginning with the eighth century, they were beginning to be a sociological phenomenon, starting to achieve complete domination under Gregory VII and Innocent III, at the time of Saint Francis.[2] This is when clericalism, the total concentration of sacred power in the hands of the clergy, emerged. The clergy monopolized the goods of salvation and became the exclusive holders of that competence necessary to produce and reproduce symbolic capital. *Pari passu* achieved a growing disaproppriation of the laity, until they were reduced to the mere mass of the faithful, attending the rites, lacking the means to produce their own religious goods.[3] Even in the language itself, this process of expropriation and concentration is operative: cleric means the learned and intellectual, and lay means uneducated and ignorant.[4]

Alongside these practices, under the sign of clericalism there developed a corresponding theology (ideology) that justified them. There is no longer reflection from the historical Jesus, powerless and at the service of others, speaking of the utopia of a community of brothers and sisters (cf. Mt 23:8), but from the oneness of God, Creator of the cosmos. This one God is represented by the one head of the pope—"God visible on earth," as Pope Gregory II said.[5] Even in christological terminology: the one invisible head of the Church, Jesus Christ, becomes visible in the pope, visible head of the Church. The Church becomes the dominion of the *monarchia sancti Petri.* This is the Church's famous theory of cephalization.[6] From the Church-communion of the people, it slowly passes to the understanding of a pyramidal Church; the Church is primarily the clergy of which the pope is the head. Before, the sacrifice of the mass was offered by all of the faithful through the priest (*tibi offerunt*); now, the priest offers it only in the name of and in place of the faithful (*pro quibus tibi offerimus*). There is introduced, definitively, the distinction between the two classes of Christians, as stated in the Code of Gratian (around 1140), father of Catholic canon law: the clergy, who receive the power of Christ, and the laity, who do not; the first are dedicated to divine service, contemplation, and prayer, free of the contamination of the world; the latter are "allowed to marry, to cultivate the earth . . . , to defend their own causes, to place offerings on the altar, to pay tithes, able to be saved if they also avoid vice and practice good works."[7] Here is verified a complete expropriation of the laity in ecclesial terms. From this there arises the interpretation that the ecclesial ministries, as practiced in the Church, are of divine institution, by the explicit will of Jesus Christ,[8] granting a proper ontological reality that other Christians do not possess and, so, are substantially unchangeable.

It is from this that clericalism, as the historical practice of the power of the clergy, gains its theoretical legitimation and its sacralization. But it is important not to forget that this process is historical, that is, it arises from within a determined structure and conjuncture, and that it should, rightly, be interpreted with the categories of the logic of power and of the mechanisms of its ideology.

The Second Vatican Council intended to return balance to the theological understanding of the distribution of power within the Church.[9] By this we would say that it meant, on the level of theological theory, the end of the age of clericalism. It established, initially, that the Church is a complete mystery, whose roots are not found in the history of humanity, but in the Holy Trinity (*ecclesia a Trinitate*); it is presented as the universal sacrament of salvation, embracing all dimensions of history, "from the just Abel to the last chosen one." In time it emerges as the people of God on the move; because the entire Church is the sacrament of Christ, Christ is represented by all; every baptized individual participates in the power (*exousia*) of Christ, of teaching, governing, and sanctifying. At the side of the christological foundation that gives stability to the Church (essential services) there is also the pneumatological foundation that responds to the historical dynamism of the ecclesial community (charisms).

In spite of this overwhelming effort, there remained in Vatican II the coexistence of the clerical principle, when the theology of a hierarchical world is expounded, without coherently taking into account what had been explained about the people of God and the participation of the faithful in the mission of Christ.[10] However, it did open a theological gap, through which passed the renewal of the distribution of sacred power in the ecclesial community.

In the first post–Vatican II era (1965–70), there arose an extraordinary effort on the part of the clergy to divest itself of the signs of power, to enter more deeply among the people, living their ministry not as someone above and beyond the faithful (priest), but as a principle of encouragement, unity, and service (ordained minister).

In the second post–Vatican age (1970–80), a strong renewal of the base of the Church occurred. Lay people began to actively participate in the life of the Church. The simple and poor people organized themselves into base Christian communities, where there is an experience of a true ecclesiogenesis.[11] Accepting the Word, formulating their prayers, and commenting on Sacred Scripture, they exercised various lay ministries, committing themselves in faith to the processes of the promotion and liberation of the oppressed. This base movement achieved, in some cases, the literal conversion of religious, priests, bishops, and cardinals, who in contact with the Christian people of these communities better redefined their ministerial service and joined in the march toward a Church of the Gospel, of service, and of commitment to the poor, and also toward a more participatory and fraternal society.[12]

In Latin America, especially, there has been a fascinating convergence: the bases request the presence of the hierarchy and religious in their ecclesial communities, accepting them in friendship and religious respect, and the hierarchy and religious, in turn, accept, support, and encourage the creation and spreading of the base communities.[13] The hierarchy gains, in this way, historical concretization, while the communities gain universality. The entire Church, more and more, ceases to be clerical, becoming a community of faith, hope, and love, a community organized under the direction of a clergy that is understood, theologically, as service within the community and not above it, gathering together, but integrating and respecting the charisms that the Risen Lord, through his Spirit, makes rise for the benefit of all.[14]

This ecclesial practice also produced its own justifying theology. It began with a reevaluation of the path of the Church through the centuries in its various forms of organization, fitting for the needs of the times, and it recommended the development of ecclesiological models that would enlighten and enrich practices along the way. Clericalism, as the appropriation of all sacred power by those who receive the sacrament of orders, appeared as a disease in need of a cure.

In the first centuries, the Church favored the communitarian pole, the Church of the *sacra communio* with an active and diverse participation by all Christians, even in the choosing of bishops and popes.[15] Later, with the rise of Christianity, the Church was organized as a *sacra potestas*, around the categories of power, which led to an exacerbated unleashing of canon law and the distorted rule of the clergy over the faithful. Today there predominates more and more the perspective of Church–People of God, fed by two saving sources: the Paschal Christ (dead and risen) and the Holy Spirit. The Christian community is born of the totality of the salvific event: it takes as its foundation the practice of the historical Jesus (*verba et facta*), his death and resurrection, and especially, the presence of the Holy Spirit. There is an immanence of the Risen Lord and of his Spirit forever within the community. It is understood as the sociohistorical location (sacrament) of the actuality of these two principles. Everyone is immersed in the Risen Lord and his Spirit. They cause to rise within the community all kinds of services, some of which seem to have a permanent character (unity and leadership by the hierarchy in the different levels of the sacrament of orders), others linked more to time and place (the various charisms). These differences are all given within the community of equals, all brothers and sisters, all sent out to witness, all responsible for ecclesial doctrine and holiness, all respecting the different manifestations of the Spirit without destroying unity.

This Church led by the Spirit and by the structuring force of charism[16] can never set its own limits; they are flexible because the reality of the Church becomes real beyond its own consciousness, especially in the situation of the poor. Objectively, independent of their moral or religious situation, by the simple fact of being poor, they are the sacrament of a special presence of Christ (cf. Mt 25:31–46), as eschatological judge who judges each one according to the love that either liberates from poverty or rejects its plea. Where Christ is, there is his Church, according to an old adage. It means, if Christ is in the poor, as he is, then there is a reality of the Church that does not depend on the faith of the poor, nor the organization of the hierarchy. The community that is born of faith in Christ and in his Spirit (Church of the Resurrection) must come to be in communion with the Church that is real in the poor (Church of the Crucifixion). And this communion is only true if it obeys the cry of Christ in the poor: "I was naked, I was hungry, I was in prison and you freed me, you fed me, and you clothed me!"[17] For the first time in history, the poor have gained ecclesiological worth and not just charitable value.

This ecclesiological theory and practice does not do away with pockets where clericalism persists. Here and there, there are still remains of a clerical structure, where the hierarchy appears comfortably on the arms of power, on the front page of the newspaper, and never among the poor, as their *defensor et procurator*, according to ancient praxis; it organizes ministry according to who is qualified, reducing the laity to a mere auxiliary force for the clergy.

Given such a structure, one must face it with the arsenal of the Gospel and not reproduce clerical systems as an easy recourse to the use of symbolic power. It is important, as is often done at the grass roots, to understand such reactions; place them in the context of the Beatitudes, never breaking away from the Shepherd when the groups, in the prophetic practice that they legitimately have within the Church, feel the need to denounce the abuses of power. More important, they must continue, positively, to work at the building of a Church that is each time more fraternal, more centered on the Gospel, and more committed to the world of the poor and to the cause of justice.

FRANCIS: OBEDIENT TO THE CHURCH OF THE POPES AND CREATOR OF A CHURCH OF THE PEOPLE

Within this context of concerns it is useful to examine the ecclesial experience of Saint Francis, to learn the lesson of Gospel freedom, and at the same time of fidelity, that he left us.[18] We find in Francis, coexisting with great tension and balance, nonconformism with obedience; acceptance of the Church of the clergy with the valiant widening of the sphere of the laity; respect for the official liturgical piety with the creativity of a popular religious culture.

The concomitance of these poles, which are not easy to articulate, allowed two currents of interpretation of Francis's attitude. The first, inaugurated by the great French Franciscan scholar Paul Sabatier,[19] emphasizes the answer of the Poverello to the Church of his time and his gradual domestication by the Roman Curia, to the point of total absorption into its clerical officiality. The second sustains the absolute obedience of the Poverello to the *sancta mater*

Ecclesia romana, because he was a *vir totus catholicus et apostolicus*, denying the thesis of a conflict between Francis and the Roman Curia supported by the writings of the saint or in the biographies of the thirteenth century; the entire life and activity of Francis is characterized by service to the Church and for the Church, making ecclesiality an essential characteristic of the Franciscan novelty.[20]

We recognize that these two tendencies have good reasons and state undeniable truths. But it is important to determine at what level each is true. We are not dealing with an easy irenism, but rather with not placing everything on the same level, thus enabling the coexistence of opposites that is the wealth of the spiritual personality of Saint Francis. He was much more than a yesman and conformist; he was a radical revolutionary and at the same time lived obedience in a heroic manner, as a form of a complete stripping of the institutional Church.

Nonconformism and Obedience

There are two levels of the experience of the Church that one must take into account. In the first place, the Church is a reality within which we find ourselves. We receive the faith, the sacraments, and Christian behavior along with our mother's milk. The Church integrates our structure, and in this way enters into the constitution of our own spiritual and religious identity. It is not as such an exterior reality, before and above us. In this perspective, it comes to us as a living organism and as charisma, as Gospel and utopia to feed our dreams and our lives.

Second, the Church emerges as a reality that surpasses us in all directions; it is before us and has a secular institutionality; it is before us and imposes itself objectively as something outside and above us. It is the Church as religious organization and as an institution with clerical characteristics. In its historical dimension it is identified with a series of options; it possesses a definite institutional profile, in this case, characterized by the centralization of sacred power, developing a certain type of doctrinal, moral, and canonical self-understanding. In short, it appears as a historical body beside other historical bodies.

These two experiences of the Church live within each of the faithful, one dominating the other without reducing, nevertheless, either one or the other. In Francis there is realized an unheard of expansion of the first experience; through him the charisma of Gospel radicalness speaks with a dawning freshness and a summer's strength. The ideals that the Church proclaims in its preaching and celebrates in its liturgical actions are perceived by Francis as something directed personally to him. The biographies of the day insist on this type of Francis's attitude. He does not hear the Gospel within himself, but rather within the context of the Church. He does not see the Church as something external to him, but rather as the atmosphere within which he breathes. On this experiential level there is not the least hint of nonconformism in Francis.

How does one place the charismatic saint of Assisi before the powerful institutionality of the Church of his time? In Saint Francis's time, beneath the papacy of Innocent III,[21] the Church achieved its highest level of secularization, with explicit interests in dominating the world. It was the Church of the *Imperium par excelence*, of the great feudal lords. More than half of all the lands of Europe were ecclesiastical holdings. The monastic life was widely feudalized; to be a monk was not to enter *in partibus pauperum*, but rather into the system of power, of lands and material goods. What characterized the monks was not the *peregrinatio evangelii*, but rather the *stabilitas loci*.[22] It is not strange, then, that the Church was more occupied with defending and administering its own goods than in evangelizing the new emerging class of artisans and merchants of the villages. The lack of evangelization made possible the rise of religious movements of deep evangelical content, led by many lay people, popular prophets, and carried-away mystics. Because of the misunderstanding or incomprehension of the local bishops, the Roman Curia, and various popes and councils (Second and Third Lateran), there was no way to channel the force of the renewing ferment for the life of the Church; the greater part of them ended by being excommunicated or were liquidated, ashamedly for the history of the Church, by the Crusades organized against them.[23]

How does Francis deal with this? He rises not from the center of power, but from the periphery. He begins his movement in a small church, the Portiuncula, which in itself constituted a symbol, because "it is the poorest of the churches of the whole region around Assisi."[24] It is on the periphery where power is not the structural parameter and the principle of control, where life flourishes in all its exuberance and as a challenge, where those who hope and live at the margin of all organization, find the necessary soil for the creativity and emergence of what is new and not yet taught. It is precisely toward the periphery that Francis directs himself. From the periphery he begins to converge on the center, calling all to conversion. The periphery is where the great prophets arise, where the reforming movements are born, and where the Spirit flourishes. The periphery possesses a theological privilege, because it is there that the Son of God was born.

Francis lives the *antithesis of the dominating endeavor of the Church*. The feudal model of Christianism, especially from the time of Gregory VII, is articulated around the two poles of the priesthood and the empire, which were in the hands of the pope and the bishops. The institutionality of the Church achieved the auger of sacred and profane power, and struggled to consolidate it, extend it, deepen it, and consecrate it with the blessings of God and of Christ as its guarantee. Never in the entire history of the Church was power sought after with such tenacity and efficiency. The clerical Church believed itself to be heir to the promises and glory of the Roman Empire (*Donatio Constantini*). On the contrary, Francis lives the plan of foolishness, the path of following the Crucified Christ in absolute poverty and simplicity. It is not a Church of lords and *maiores* that seduces him, but rather a Church of the servants, of the *minores*. His order will be called that of the "lesser brothers,"[25] without any power over themselves, much less over others;[26] everything that signifies power should be denied to the group, to the point that in the *Regula non-bullata* there is prescribed the exclusion of works that imply positions of command, such as "bankers, foremen, administrators in the houses in which they serve."[27] To that point, Joseph Ratzinger says: "Francis's no to that type of Church could not be more radical. It is what we would call a prophetic protest."[28] To the Gospel of power Francis opposes the power of the Gospel. He never tolerated his brothers assuming prelacies or posts in the Church: "Their vocation is to remain below, following the footsteps of Christ; if you want [he says to a bishop] them to give fruit in the Church of God, let them remain in their vocation, keeping them in humble positions, even against their will."[29]

Francis also lived the *antithesis of clericalism.* We should never lose sight of the fact that he was a lay person and wanted to remain such to evangelize the laity who were pastorally abandoned, above all the poor. If later he became an ordained lay person, it was with the aim of being able to preach with greater liberty, since there was a conciliar prohibition that disallowed the preaching by lay people on doctrinal matters.[30] He was never an agent of the clerical system. The astute historian Eduardo Hoornaert[31] calls attention to the mistaken perspective of considering Francis a man of the Church, that is, a cleric with influence among the people. Even today his image is in harmony with the popular culture almost everywhere, especially in northeastern Brazil, where he has penetrated deeply into the soul of the people,[32] in their folklore and artisan culture.

Francis lived in the same way the *antithesis of the religious monastic life* of the time. His life was characterized by stability and autonomy. Beginning with the reform of Cluny, the monks no longer did manual labor in the country; they became feudal lords with their colonies, charging tithes, rents of the farmlands and mills, and tributes from the servants of the region. Everything had its place within the walls of the monasteries, small earthly Jerusalems, mirrors of heaven. Evangelization took place from there, a center of power and culture. Francis is the initiator of a religious life in the midst of the people, his cell is the world, his brothers are all people, primarily the poor. They wander from city to city, two by two, announcing a Gospel without interpretations or picturesque commentaries proper to the exegesis of the day. They live from the work of each day, in poverty, simplicity, and joy.

Francis markedly lives the *antithesis of the learned culture* of the time. Preaching was done in Latin, a language the people did not understand, and accompanied by speaking in allegories that hid and weakened its strength. Francis proclaims the Gospel *ad litteram.* If he allows study of the Sacred Scriptures it is with a very precise condition: "That it not be studied only to know how to speak, but rather to practice what they have heard, and practicing it they offer to others to do likewise."[33] He wants his brothers not to be followers of this or that school, but rather to be "disciples of the Gospel, in a special way that they progress in truth and at the same time they grow in purity and simplicity."[34] He considers himself an "idiot," that is, illiterate, with respect to culture, because he can read and write only with great difficulty.[35]

Francis also lives the *antithesis of the legal spirit* of his day. Deeply committed to temporal power and historical leadership, the Church felt the need for law, which structurally has the function of ordering and legitimating practices of power in the course of relating with other powers. In effect, beginning in the twelfth century, a rich canonical reflection was developed that found in Gratian a codifier of genius. Ecclesiology was developed from the law, especially around the papacy and its attributes. This canon law, as we have already pointed out, had ordered the *corpus christianorum* into classes: on the one hand, the clergy, who have to do with everything religious; on the other, the laity, totally stripped. Francis opens the doors of his movement to all without distinction. Becoming "lesser brothers," all differences of origin disappear; all, be they priests, nobles, merchants, lawyers, bourgeoisie, or servants, enter a fraternity of radically fraternal equality.[36] Not only the men are called to this radical following of the Gospel; Francis's movement is also open to the women, who, beginning with Clare and Ines, also live the radicalness of poverty, without demanding any dowry or gift that would guarantee their livelihood. They also live from their work and from alms. Faced with the hierarchical vision of the Christian community, Francis proposes the fraternal model patterned after the Knights of the Round Table.

Francis lives the *antithesis of paternalism and monarchism in the institutional structure of the Church.* The practice of power led to the concentration in the hands of the clergy of the means of religious production. The justifying understanding needed for this practice was developed; here, categories of the most ancient imperial tradition came into play, managed by a political theology whose roots are found in Egypt and the Middle East. The one God-Father is represented by the monarch, father of his people. All the rest are subordinate, organized in a descending hierarchy; it is the kingdom of children. The relationship of the children among themselves is not developed, which would open up the opportunity for the idea of fraternity, but only the relationship of the children to the one father. Consequently, there is produced an inflating of the principle of the father, which generates patriarchism from the idea of the fullness of power in only one person. The Church, rooted in this model of political monarchism, appears as a society in principle, unequal and hierarchical.[37]

Francis lives another experience of faith, tied to the most authentic sources of the New Testament. Because he is poor and unarmed and does not try to impose himself on others, but rather to serve them, he discovers the radical fraternity of all beings. God does not cease being Father. But this Father has one Son who is His substantial image and the only representative of the Father. This Son became human and mixed with God's adopted children. He was the great Brother among brothers. Francis lives this experience of Christ as Brother.[38] From there comes the discovery of the umbilical cord that unites all human beings, the understanding of the Church as fraternity and as universal confraternization blossoms. All represent the Father to the degree to which they are the children in the Son who is among us; this representation is no longer monopolized by anyone, and if by chance it persists (as a certain understanding of the ecclesial apostolates), it must be lived within the community and among the brothers and not above them. In this context of ideas the petition of Francis arises in all its logic: "May no one call himself 'prior' among us, but rather that all be called without distinction 'lesser brothers,' washing the feet of one another";[39] and immediately afterward adding well-known Gospel texts against power (cf. Mt 20:25–26; Lk 22:26), he delegitimizes the principle of power as a relationship between the brothers and others, equally brothers, substituting for it the principle of mutual service.[40] This experience has profound ecclesiological consequences because it translates the mystery of the Church into categories of the practice of Jesus, and not into those of the monarchism and monotheism of the Old Testament and of the political theologies of ancient imperialism.

As can be seen, we are faced with a radical nonconformism by Francis, but a practical nonconformism, and not just words. Francis does not develop, theoretically, an alternative model for being Christian; as "ignorant and idiot," illiterate, not having gone through the school of *ius canonicum* and *sacra doctrina*, he would be incapable of such a thing. Because of this, his is not an answer according to modern criteria, because he does not start from an alternative theoretical understanding of the Church and society, and from this move to corresponding practices. Francis deeply respects the structure that he finds. His declared love and his unrestricted obedience to the Church and to the pope in the exordium of the two remaining rules and in his *Testament*, his veneration for priests, no matter how poor and undignified they were[41]—these are neither rhetorical tricks nor diversionary tactics. He is profoundly sincere and loyal. But this obedience does not keep him from also obeying the charism that God caused to burst forth in him. His intuition about the truth of faith and of the Gospel allows him to understand that no form of the Church exhausts the entire mystery of the Church. Each historical form concretizes the strength of the Gospel, because of which it must be respected and loved. However, the Gospel is greater than history; because of this, it brings forth the freedom to go beyond the ecclesial concretization, not against it or in spite of it, but precisely beyond it. In the face of death, he lucidly recommends "to guard poverty and fidelity to the Roman Church, but, above all other dispositions, fidelity to the Holy Gospel."[42] The Gospel is the ultimate root for the entire Church and for each Christian, as for the lay Francis.

There is, then, an undeniable nonconformism in Saint Francis; his plan is not within the institutionality of the day; it is a Gospel plan. But he is a man of the Spirit in such a way that he realizes that the Gospel is not the monopoly of anyone, not even he, Francis; nor of the feudal and imperial Church. The Gospel is a ferment that continually gives life to the whole body, penetrating the institutional form as well as the charismatic moment of the community.

Overcoming all aspects of Pharisaism, the evangelical love of Francis allows him to love the Church with its deep limitations, above all in that which has to do with the evangelization of the poor. This love is not easy; nor is it free of tensions. In his *Testament*, when already near death, he could confess: "No one showed me what I had to do, but rather the Most High Himself revealed to me that I had to live according to the way of the Holy Gospel."[43] Francis was a gift of God to his Church. It received him not without apprehensions, as it did in an exaggerated way with previous evangelical movements, the great majority of whom, not free of blame for their inflexibility and the worldliness of the Roman Curia, condemned and marginated from the ecclesial community.[44] "The fact that the institution would doubt, distrusting and trying to re-

duce the original radicalness," says Tadeo Matura, "shows the re-
action of someone who feels threatened. The final acceptance of
Franciscan evangelism on the part of the Church shows, however,
that answering and adding to liberty form part of its deepest being,
in that, far from destroying, it renews the Church."[45]

Francis understood his vocation as a servant of the Church and
not as somebody in opposition to it. He believed that he heard
Christ himself speak to him in the church of San Damiano: "Francis, go and repair my Church, which as you see is in ruins."[46] He
lived his vocation not to back the ecclesial endeavor for power,
because this would not have been to repair the Church but to have
left it as it was. The recreation of the theological substance of the
Church comes from cutting itself off from the sources of ecclesial
faith, that is, from the Gospel and the following of the poor and
humble Christ. This is what Francis intuitively did. That the Church
understood this is demonstrated, in the symbolic language of
dreams, by the attitude of Innocent III; according to the legend,
the pope saw in his dream the Church of the Lateran, "mother and
head of all the churches," on the verge of collapse. But, "a religious, small and insignificant, held it up on his shoulders so that
it did not fall. 'Certainly,' he said, 'this is the one who in word and
action will hold up the Church of Christ.' "[47] Innocent III, sensitive
to the needs of the times and understanding the pauperistic movements, as opposed to his predecessors Alexander III and Lucius III,
who condemned them because they felt threatened by them, approved the plan of Francis and his companions in 1209–10. This
approval not only started the flourishing of a new order in the
Church, but the re-creation of the Church itself at its base, especially among the poor. This is what we will try to explain further.

A Church of the Base with the Poor
To understand Francis's ecclesiogenesis, it is necessary to take
into account the extraordinary consciousness that he had of his
own mission. There is a curious paradox in his own life: on the one
hand, he is the "least of all the servants," "useless and unworthy
creature of the Lord God," who "kisses the feet of all," submissive
to "every human creature," including the animals themselves;[48]
and, on the other hand, he manifests the understanding of his his-
toric-salvific importance: he laces his own words with those of

Christ,[49] and also has a salvific strength (*ad salvationem animae nostrae*);[50] they will be called on the day of judgment[51] and will preserve their truthfulness until the end of the world (*nunc et semper donec fiierit mundus iste*);[52] he speaks to all Christians, "to all who live in the universal world," to "all the mayors, consuls, judges, and governors of the entire world";[53] the *Testament* that he leaves he understands in a biblical sense, as a covenant, in the line of Moses and Christ.[54] If Francis had not balanced this religious hubris with the constant confession of his littleness and insignificance, we would say that we were dealing with a serious pathological condition. But the truth is that we find ourselves faced with a Christian genius of seductive humanity and fascinating gentleness, which causes us to discover what is most true in our humanity.

This same paradox also becomes patent in this experience with the Church; on the one hand, he is most faithful to the Church that he finds and in which he lives: "Brother Francis promises obedience and reverence to the Lord Pope Honorius";[55] as well as following the footsteps of Christ, he proposes "to follow the venerated footsteps of the holy Church,"[56] and he asks that "all the brothers be Catholic and live and speak in accord with Catholic doctrine."[57] On the other hand, he has a clear understanding that he was sent to recreate the Church according to the spirit of the Sermon on the Mount and in the sense of the poor.

The most famous text of his ecclesiogenesis has been preserved for us by the *Legend of Perugia* and the *Mirror of Perfection*, and according to critics, has a secure historical root:[58] "The religion and life of the "lesser brothers" is a small congregation that the Son of God has asked of his heavenly Father in these recent times, begging him: I would like, Father, that you be so kind as to grant me a new and humble people now, who through their humility and poverty are different from those who have gone before them, and that they have as their only pleasure the possession of me alone." And the heavenly Father answered his beloved Son: "My Son, may it be done. . . . It is a great thing that the Lord would want to have a new and humble people, who have nothing in common in their life and maxims with those who have gone before them, and who are content with having only the Most High and Glorious Lord as their own."[59]

Francis defines his movement, in consonance with this text, in the same terms with which we define the Church: small flock (*pusillus grex*) and new people (*populus novus*). In fact, he did not intend to found an order with its own structure and mission within the Church. His primary intention was to live what every baptized individual is called to realize: the following of Jesus Christ oriented by the ethos of the Gospel. Francis's ideal consists in wanting to remain at the base (*in plano subistere*),[60] not in introducing a new body into the Church beside those already in existence. He wanted to live the mystery of the Church, which is the mystery of the poor and humble Jesus. But, faced with the dynamic and structural intentionality of the imperial Church of the time, he was conscious of the novelty of his style of life. Founding communities of poor people, his purpose was not in starting an *ecclesiola* within the *Ecclesia*, but rather in giving spark to that which is called to be the Church in the following of the poor Christ, that is, a Church of the poor, poor and naked. The *Sacrum Commercium* makes this purpose one of its central themes: the function of the poor and fraternal community of Francis is to realize the Church of the poor, which belongs only to God because it is stripped of all earthly goods (that is why it is poor), and because it is free of all property and lives only by that which is indispensable for raw existence.[61] All of the original biographical literature is oriented toward the thesis that the movement of Francis is the manifestation of a renewed Church, made real in three branches: that of the men, that of the women, and that of the penitents. It does not deal, then, with the creation of a new Church, which cannot be created except that Christ and the Spirit founded it, but rather of causing an ecclesiogenesis, that is, granting a new expression to the christological and pneumatological essence of the Church. And this expression, distinct from that of his time, must be poor and humble.

Francis understands the two expressions of the Church, rich and poor, as two different forms of the manifestation of the same Christ. In the rich Church there is the Christ who gives and aids the poor with his goods (*Christus largiens*); in the poor Church is the Christ who receives and is aided (*Christus accipiens*). Francis's novelty consisted in having understood the necessity of the poor Church for the age, characterized by the breakdown of the feudal system, the emergence of a new historical subject (the bourgeoisie), with the liberation of the countless poor reduced by the two systems.

These poor demanded a specific evangelization, an experience of church adequate to their situation. Francis articulated this ecclesiogenesis. But he did not close himself off in his own living of the Church; he also embraced the other manifestation of the mystery of the Church. Because of this, living together within him, dialectically, there are the two fidelities: to the Church of the lord pope and to the Church of the poor, both integrating the one mystery of the Church. Let us look at some characteristics of Francis's ecclesiogenesis.

A Church of Fraternal Relationships

We have already accentuated in many places the importance of the fraternity for Francis. Relationships must not be hierarchical, from the unequal distribution of power, but absolutely fraternal, everyone being brothers and sisters, even where there are different functions, as it says in the *Regula non-bullata:* brothers who preach, pray, work, clerics and lay;[62] that there be no prior, but rather ministers and servants. This fraternity, which gives shape to the Church, must be open to all without distinction, even "to thief or robber, to friend or adversary."[63] The possible ministries that arise or emerge from within the group do not carry with them any special privilege. The priests and the nonclerics are equal in the Franciscan rules. Francis resists entering the clerical sphere common in his day. His entire movement, including those who had entered as priests, must be considered an auxiliary force of the Church in ministry: "We have been sent to aid the clergy (*ad adjutorium clericorum*) in the salvation of souls, to help them in whatever they themselves cannot do."[64] The later clericalization of the order, even today, comes from motives other than those of Francis, at its insertion into the clerical rule of the Church.

A Church That Is Fed by the Word

That which calls forth fraternity is the hearing of the Word, the following of the poor Christ, and solidarity with the poor. It is not a markedly sacramental piety that is notable in Francis, but there is in him a gentle love for the Eucharist that prolongs the humility of the Incarnation. He visited as many churches as he could and received communion often.[65] But the novelty, in a Church with a relaxed, semiignorant clergy, given little to reflection upon the

Gospel, consists in the love for the Word of Revelation. All of the texts of the saint are penetrated by it. "Francis's highest aspiration his most living desire, and his most elevated purpose was to observe in everything and always the Holy Gospel . . . in constant meditation he remembered its words and with the sharpest clarity they permeated his works."[66] His deep penetration into the meaning of the Scriptures was well known, especially because he did not have book learning;[67] it is that he saw with the heart. In his doubts he consulted the Gospel; all his preaching was nothing but the announcement of the Gospel; he divided the only copy of the New Testament so that all the brothers could meditate upon it; he asked that no one step on paper that was thrown on the ground because of his respect for the sacred words that they might contain, and he collected them with great veneration and care.[68] Like our base Christian communities, so also the fraternities of the first brothers were structured around the Word and the following of the poor Christ.

A Church of Mutual Aid

The poor fraternity is supported not by material goods, but by mutual charity and sensitivity to the needs of one another. In this context, Francis introduces a maternal element into the community. Each one must be a mother to the other,[69] attentive to needs and illness. This help is not reduced to material necessities, but also comprehends interior problems. The brothers should be open to one another with confidence, confessing to one another, joyful for the good that God accomplishes in each one.[70] Through preaching and good example all of us become spouses, brothers and mothers of Jesus Christ;[71] even "my little poor brother who did not receive in the Church the power to have children" becomes a mother who gives life to others through prayer.[72]

A Church that Celebrates Life

Francis was a profoundly sacramental person in the sense that he intuitively created gestures and meaningful acts. His own idea of following Jesus tended toward representation and dramatization of the life and attitudes of the historical Jesus. The celebration of faith was not restricted, for him, to liturgical celebrations. He did not pray, like monks, only within some sacred place; his experience of God took place in the world, in contact with people, the poor, and nature. The different prayers that he left display this profound creativity. In his preaching, "he used simple subjects and comparisons . . . , and with gestures and burning expressions he carried his listeners away." The stock accounts of the biographers are filled with the language of gestures: dressing himself like a beggar and asking alms in French, having himself be led by a cord around his neck through the streets for having eaten a bit of chicken while he says: "Look at this glutton who ate meat without you knowing it";[73] dancing in a pilgrim's outfit on Easter; putting ashes in his food or sprinkling them over his head to give a lesson in humility to his brothers. He celebrates life like a liturgy, because he finds traces of God, of Christ, or passages of the Gospel in everything. The "Canticle of Brother Sun" shows a new meaning of prayer in contact with life and its dramas.

A Church of Popular Religiosity

Identified with the world of the poor, Francis accepts the poor's universe of representation. This is organized by means of the logic of the subconscious and is expressed by way of symbols. Francis's entire language is laden with archetypal symbolism. The mysteries of Jesus are represented by him in a concrete manner, very much in the way of the people. Thus, he was the one who introduced the living celebration of Christmas through the manger scene,[74] with the sheep, the ox, and the donkey. His devotion to the humanity of Christ made him begin to paint the Crucified Christ, no longer on foot, triumphant, but in agony, with the signs of suffering and torture. The Way of the Cross was promoted thanks to the presence of the Franciscans in the holy places of Palestine.[75] Devotion to the Immaculate Virgin Mary, to the angels, especially Saint Gabriel, and to all who were related to the humanity of Jesus received decisive emphasis from Francis. The indulgence of the Portiuncula (the "pardon of Assisi," as it is also called) is tied to his gentle devotion to Mary. He also demonstrates a great creativity, besides his profound respect, with liturgical piety; he composes an office of the Passion, so that the brothers might pray it along with the canonical office; he does an interpretation of the Lord's Prayer; he introduces the celebration of the mass among the people, with the advantage of the portable altar, which was a novelty in his time.[76] A breeze of the people, simple, colorful, and refreshing, blows through the windows of the old and secular Christian edifice of the thirteenth century, thanks to the liberty of Francis. This freedom achieved its greatest expression when, in the face of death, he celebrated his last supper with his brothers. Although he was only a deacon, he acted out the Last Supper of Jesus, as a type of celebration and covenant: "He commanded them to bring bread, he blessed it, he broke it and gave it to his followers."[77] Celano comments that "he did all of this in memory of the supper of the Lord, and to make manifest the love he had for the brothers."[78]

A Missionary Church

The spreading of the community around Francis, even in his lifetime, throughout almost all of Europe, is extraordinary. After ten years, there were already more than three thousand brothers, and according to some sources the number is five thousand.[79] The chroniclers of the time confirm that they filled the world and that there was no province of Christianity in which they were not present.[80] They went two by two through the villages and cities, and soon arrived in France, Germany, Hungary, and England. The causes of this expansion were many, the principle one being the impact of the image of Francis and the answer his message and his life style gave to the expectations of his time. Jacobo de Vitry, a cardinal friend of the brothers, says precisely: "This order has spread with such speed throughout the earth because it imitates with such decisiveness the life of the primitive Church and the apostles."[81] The *Chronicon Normanniae* is right in affirming that the spreading of the Franciscan fraternity is owed, over all, to the "totally new way of life of its members" that constituted a great attraction for youth.[82] But the principal reason for this is the missionary spirit of Francis and of his first companions; they understood their vocation as a divine mandate to revitalize the Church. As we have already stated, they did not understand themselves as a group apart, but rather as a part of a Church renewed by the breath of the Gospel. Because of this, the primitive Franciscan community was essentially missionary, as is the entire Church.

A Church as Sacrament of the Spirit

Wherever so much spontaneity and creativity blossoms, where maternal attitudes of care and gentleness are called forth for others, it is natural that there lives the powerful presence of the Holy

Spirit, source of all life and feminine principle of salvation.[83] Francis is seen as a man of the Spirit par excellence,[84] and his spirituality is based on the clearest sources of the Spirit.[85] There is in Francis a twofold discovery: the holy humanity of Jesus and the decisive presence of the Spirit of the Lord.[86] It was not for no reason that he wanted the Holy Spirit to be the minister general of the order.[87] For Francis, the Spirit of the Lord produces two fundamental freedoms: the liberation of the old man, centered in the ego, with his vices, with his "desire to impose himself on others,"[88] and, overall, the liberation for others in mutual love and service, in the unrestricted surrender to the Father, in the obedience to the movements of the Spirit, who works wonders. The liberty lived by Francis, within a deep sense of adherence to the theological substance of the Church and tradition, has its origin in his experience of the Spirit.[89] The community is the carrier of this Spirit; because of this, Francis deeply respects the path of each individual and asks the brothers that they respect one another because of the presence of the Spirit. The ecclesial community, taking shape in the Franciscan community, will be thus converted into a sacrament of the Spirit.

A Fully Catholic Church

The incarnation of the community among the poor, living the Gospel in the concrete place of the poor, can become a risk to an essential dimension of the Church, its catholicity and universality. Because of their way of life, because of their basic options, the followers of Francis had much in common with the popular evangelical movements of the age, which were afterward considered to be heretical. They understood themselves in terms of their fascination with Francis and they joined the Franciscan movement, adding to its unity. The more the Church is particularized, the more it needs explicit references to the center of unity, the pope, in order to insure its universality. This is what Francis did, led by his catholic instinct. Because of this he says in the *Regula non-bullata:* "All of the brothers must be Catholic and live and speak like Catholics. But if one should stray from Catholic life and faith in word or deed, may he be completely excluded from the fraternity."[90] Obedience to the pope and his successors means to insure from the beginning the universal perspective. The almost inquisitorial way, in the *Tes-*

tament, in which he commands the brothers who do not act as Catholics to be punished[91] leads one to believe in the existence of serious problems of orthodoxy within the order. This reference to Rome is not only juridical and doctrinal, but also has an emotional aspect, with the presence of the cardinal protector of the order and with the recitation of the canonical hours in conformity with the chapel at the pope's palace in the Lateran.[92] These demonstrations of fidelity are not servile, because Francis continues on his path of simplicity and identification with the poor. However, this transcendence toward the nonworld does not allow him to lose the meaning of the world of the institutional Church, which is accepted as a necessary fact for the Catholic path. And so, his catholicity is total, because it is not limited to a mere institutional fidelity, but is open to what is below, toward a theological fidelity to the presence of Christ in the people and in the poor whom he serves and with whom he shares his fraternity.

THE ECCLESIAL EXPERIENCE OF SAINT FRANCIS AND OUR OWN ECCLESIOGENESIS

Francis's ecclesial experience is extraordinarily suggestive for the times in which we live. More and more, the Church, as a totality, is moving from the center to the periphery. It gradually is entering into the world of the poor, making it possible for them also to feel that they are Church, and it is entering into the particularities of each region; thus, the local Church is given value. This incarnational process is only possible with great Gospel courage and freedom of Spirit, as in the case of Francis of Assisi. He did not have a spiritual director; nor did he follow a previously marked path. His guide was the Gospel, his teacher Jesus Christ, and his inspiration the Holy Spirit. Bishops, cardinals, and popes came into his life because they were necessary for the legitimation of his path, never for the purpose of privileges and dispensations.[93] He remained free of books and far from the great monastic rules consecrated by history. He had a consciousness of his originality and the risk of his enterprise. He never lost height or sense of direction; because of this, he could live together with an imperial, and in some respects scandalous, Church. Never did he deny the monopoly of the goods of salvation, nor the aptitude of the priestly body, as simonious as it was. But not because of this did he cease to follow his path, which *in practice* meant the production and distribution of the goods of salvation in a new way, within the other distribution of sacred power, in his case circular, egalitarian, and fraternal. How could he maintain this tension without being destroyed by it? Because of his Gospel spirit.

The Church carries within itself constant tension: it proclaims what it can never put into practice, the utopia of the Kingdom and radical fraternity among all people. It was precisely these values that Francis lived: the man of the Gospel, sincere, simple, and authentic, but radical to the greatest degree, which always allowed him to be obedient to the Church of tradition as well as to the Church of the poor. Although with different signs, the two Churches live the same desire of fidelity to the Gospel. Francis did not opt for the Church of imperialism of the feudal popes, but rather for the Church of the mistreated and lowly. However, he respected, venerated, and also considered the Church of Rome to be his own. He never detracted from it; nor did he allow that the defects and sins of its ministers be pointed out because "I recognize in them the Son of God and they are my lords. And I do so because of this: because in this world I see nothing corporal of the Son of the Most High Himself except for His Most Holy Body and Blood that they receive and only they administer to others."[94] His strategy was not backhanded, but rather one of conquest through goodness and the radicalness of living the Gospel. When someone is evangelic and puts up even with persecution on the part of the Church in the spirit of the Beatitudes, remaining united to it and loving it ("although they persecute me, I want to have recourse to the priests"),[95] then there is no way of excluding him or her from the ecclesial community, just as there is no way of stopping him or her from renovation and innovation within the Church.

Francis always maintained these two fidelities, to the poor and to the ecclesial institution; he never leaned toward one or the other pole. Because of this he could give meaning to both: to the poor, bringing them to the message of the Gospel, consoling them and joining with them in ecclesial communities; to the ecclesial institution, disquieting it with the Gospel, and understanding his own charism as a treasure of the Church and not belonging to him alone.

Whenever it finds the paths of the poor, and in the path of the poor becomes one with them, accepting them as one accepts Christ, the Church realizes its own essence and experiences faithfulness to its Lord, who became poor in this world and wanted to be served through the poor to save all people.

In light of the ecclesial praxis of Francis, the path of the Church maintains its course with the oppressed, and in this valley of the tears of the poor, it proclaims and waits for the promised land.

With his practice, Francis demonstrated that the theological substance of the Church is not exhausted or even captured within the official institution. The Church is not realized only by means of the ministries, rites, canons, and doctrines; in a word, by means of the educational institution. It is realized also, and principally, when people allow themselves to be fed by the Word of God. Then, they are united; they discover themselves as children of God and brothers and sisters among themselves; they commit themselves to the following of Christ and place themselves at the service of others. In other words, the Church is also an event. The event does not have permanence in the cohesion of the institution; it bursts forth, producing a human and religious meaning, and can disappear to blossom in some other way, at some other time. Event means the presence of the Spirit in the community; it is the strength of the charism that recovers the flavor of newness and transparency of the Gospel, which in the form of the institution of the Church runs the risk of becoming opaque tradition and repetition. Because Francis embraced both forms of the concretization of the Church—as institution and as event—he truly could be called *vir totus catholicus et apostolicus.*

·5

Integration of the Negative

THE CONTRIBUTION OF SAINT FRANCIS TO THE PROCESS OF INDIVIDUATION

I heard an aged confrere, wise and good, perfect and holy, say: If you feel the call of the Spirit, then be holy with all your soul, with all your heart, and with all your strength.

If, however, because of human weakness you cannot be holy, then be perfect with all your soul, with all your heart, and with all your strength.

But, if you cannot be perfect because of vanity in your life, then be good with all your soul, with all your heart, and with all your strength.

Yet, if you cannot be good because of the trickery of the Evil One, then be wise with all your soul, with all your heart, and with all your strength.

If, in the end, you can be neither holy, nor perfect, nor good, nor wise because of the weight of your sins, then carry this weight before God and surrender your life to His divine mercy.

If you do this, without bitterness, with all humility, and with a joyous spirit due to the tenderness of a God who loves the sinful and ungrateful, then you will begin to feel what it is to be wise, you will learn what it is to be good, you will slowly aspire to be perfect, and finally you will long to be holy.

If you do all this, with all your soul, with all your heart, and with all your strength, then I assure you, my brother, you will be on the path of Saint Francis, you will not be far from the Kingdom of God.

Within every great saint there lives a great demon. The roots of sanctity are born in the depths of human frailty. Virtues are great because temptations conquered were great. One is not nursed on sanctity like mother's milk during infancy. Behind the saint is hidden a person who has conquered the hells of human nature and the crush of sins, despair, and the denial of God. They have fought with God like Jacob (Gn 23) and they have been marked by the battle. Because of this, it is foolish and unthinking to imagine the life of a saint as carefree, easy, and clear-cut. Sainthood is the reward for a painful battle that has been won.

Within every heart abide angels and demons; a volcanic passion shows itself in every human action; life and death instincts abound within every person; desires to reach out, desires of communion with others and of self-giving live alongside the urges of selfishness, of rejection, of meanness. This is especially true in the lives of the saints. If they are saints, it is because they sense all of this not as destructive, but rather, overcoming them by facing them, checking and channeling them toward the good. It is not without reason that the saints represent the best in the human race. No one can take away from the fascination and the secret challenge they give us.

This agonizing[1] situation can be observed especially in the person of Saint Francis, considered the first after the Only Son, Jesus Christ.[2] As a result of our reflections, we see that Francis was, by the work and grace of the Mysterious, a *vir desideriorum*, that is, a man possessed by the power of desire, ignited by the volcano of Eros and Pathos. The ancients as well as the moderns would say that the Poverello was inhabited by a powerful daimon or by an especially beneficent genius.[3] He is seen as a polarized "force of nature" in communion and identification with nature, with the poor, with the Crucified One, and with God, a power that shines brightly even in our day.

By their very nature, Eros and Pathos—because they constitute the basic energy of human life—expand in all directions. Because of this, we must always recognize that, as a force, they lend themselves as much to constructive as to destructive purposes. They may overcome individuals, possessing them, as the highest expressions of love as well as the lowest expressions of hatred. Love and hate are articulations of the same personality; it is the same energy that runs through one and the other, although in differing directions. Freud demonstrated well that it is apathy that is in opposition to Pathos, just as indifference opposes love (Eros). With reason, the woman Diatima, in Plato's dialogue of the *Banquet*, says she is the Eros of a daimon, that is to say, a power that can be angelic as well as demonic, a fact we can readily see in our artists, lovers, and saints, or in our famous villains, fanatic leaders, and the insane. The coexistence of these two poles does not have to be self-destructive. It can and should, however, be channeled and given direction. We have already reflected upon the primary function of the Logos (rationality or the structure of meaning): to domesticate the daimon, to give it direction without imprisoning it in the net of its own channeling. Because of this, the reason and plan for liberation must face an adversary that abides in life: the opposite pole of Eros and Pathos. As a result, temptations always present themselves in the form of the unrealized possibilities of Eros and Pathos. Great virtues are, then, accompanied by terrible temptations. This is not so much because of extrahuman forces, but because of the very essence of the passion of life.

When the Logos is able to channel these energies without denying them, then gentleness blossoms, the compassion and care that give light and flavor to human existence. But there are different paths and ways of relating Eros and Logos within the scope of what it means to be holy.

THE SAINT: A PERFECT OR INTEGRATED PERSON?

The question we want to reflect upon here is: What is the most adequate and human attitude in the face of the radical ambiguity of passion? In other words, what behavior best attempts to expand one's identity and best widens the borders of freedom? There are two strategies that present themselves as *idealtypus* and result in two types of saints: one perfect and the other integrated. One follows the model of channelization, and the other the model of consolidation; one is described by the image of an arrow that flies toward a target, and the other by the figure of a circle that surrounds and integrates.

A strategy of channelization means that Eros and Pathos are accepted in their demonic strength, but only to the degree to which they support some rational plan of action. There is the risk, which could be fatal, that the aspects that enter into what we call perfection may be repressed, denied, and rejected. This does not mean that the denied forces disappear or cease to exist. They are present as they are: denied and unaccepted. They constantly try to emerge, trying to convince the consciousness of their right to existence. The more one tries to control them, the greater is the risk that Eros and Pathos may need to be faced consciously. This is the model utilized in the search for perfection through the development of the virtues. The aspects of light, goodness, and positiveness are dealt with directly. The other shadow dimensions that also belong to human reality are continually brought under control. Post-Tridentine Christianity (from the sixteenth century to the present) is dominated by this type of Christian ideal and sanctity. It is a tribute to modernism, under the domination of the rational. The Christian saint is in perfect control of all instincts; one's ideal of perfection is pursued inflexibly; any passion that is opposed to the virtues is put down and repressed. The Christian saint is perfect, but rigid, hard, and at times heartless. There is no gentleness in many modern saints. Instead, there is impeccable perfection, achieved at the expense of what is human in attitude and relationships.

The way of integration follows another path. It tries to assume all of the complexities of Eros and Pathos. The function of reason is crucial to every living being, to basic intuition, to all of the other aspects of human passion. Nothing is rejected, but every aspect of life is made to circle like satellites orbiting around some central point. The primary effort lies in attaining balance. The passions are not feared, but are accepted as natural; they are dealt with, without being denied. Thus, the accepted negativity loses its virulence and behaves like a house pet. The liberated energy strengthens the positive pole, the goal of the saint. The result is the profile of every saint: an integrated individual, master of his energies because they are within his reins; he is capable of gentleness and of deeply human acts because he is not held back by simple rationality or by blind control. As Rollo May recognized: "To be able to feel and live fully the capacity for gentle love demands a confrontation with the demonic. The two appear to be opposed, but if one is denied, the other is also lost."[4] To make sure that this integration is not the result of some theoretic synthesis, one must know and experience the angels and the demons that inhabit life. Integration is the result of many comings and goings, ups and downs, acceptances and denials, until it crystallizes as a powerful center that attracts and harmonizes all.[5] When the saint considers himself to be a vile sinner, unworthy of salvation or of God, he speaks the truth, because he is speaking of the shadow aspects, those sinister ones that are the demons that reign within us. In the plan for holiness, these are controlled, but not dead, and they are always integrated so that their strength may not destroy us, but rather help us to arrive at the promised land of our own being.

Francis was a saint who integrated the totality of his energies in an archetypal way. The negative especially was included as a way of harmony in every direction, wherever it might have been aimed. We want to emphasize some aspects of this integration of the negative, because we have already treated the positive in Chapter 1. We believe that Francis—with his perfect joy, with his path of joyful humility, lived within the dark night of the senses and spirit— may evoke in us unsuspected powers of harmony and conquest within our own heart.

There is a certain amount of suffering, misunderstanding, and existential absurdity that is inherent in human life, as we all know. Each of us passes through crises that offer us the chance to grow or that may become enormous traumas.[6] All humans must resolve their Oedipus complex, that is to say, attain their autonomy and be their own person, something that becomes a fine drama for some and a tragedy for others. No one can spend one's entire life avoiding the great question of personal death, neglecting to define oneself in terms of the meaning of human hope. To treat these questions is more than to elaborate some theory that is then simply forgotten. It means to build a path that must be traveled day by day, without illusions and with a sober resignation (*ataraxia*) that is the expression of the wisdom of an adult spirit.

Contemporary humanity has made unheard of progress in the understanding of those mechanisms that produce suffering, especially those concerned with social injustice; we have produced thousands of ways of protecting life, therapeutic techniques for all our psychological pathologies, and an immense pharmacy in order to wipe out or alleviate pain. But, in spite of this, there is nothing to say that we know better than medieval society how to face the problem of existence and to set out a *modus vivendi* that will assure reasons for living and the joy of living with others. Within this context, perhaps Francis of Assisi may be able to illuminate us.

THE SYM-BOLIC AND THE DIA-BOLIC AS PATHS TO GOD

We want to shed some light here on a few significant points about the exuberant biography of Francis that show his sharing of life with "brother dia-bolic" who accompanies "brother sym-bolic"[7] on the path of life. The biographies and the stories of the time are replete with the words of Francis, wherein he is humble with himself, confesses himself to be a sinner and the unworthy servant of others.[8] He commanded his intimate friend Brother Leo to record: "Brother Francis, you have been so evil, your sins make you worthy only of hell."[9] Other times, he asked that he be trampled on by one whom he had offended. His conception or idea of minority implicated gestures that translated or completely lowered the *I*, as if to leave it behind, or to be joyful in the face of offenses, misunderstandings, and calumnies, to assert joyfully that "he was a despicable man by outward appearances, small in stature, and because of this was considered to be a vile poor man whom no one noticed."[10] When a confrère asked him: "Father, what do you think of yourself?" he answered: "I know that I am the worst sinner because, if God had shown some criminal all of the mercy He has shown to me, that man would be twice as spiritual as I am."[11]

Such self-knowledge is a powerful blow against all narcissism.[12] The *I* and its desire to affirm itself never tries to recognize its negative counterpart, but hides it and even denies it. Francis, with this explicit ownership of the diabolic, liberates himself for a total experience of his own reality and so allows for an integration without rejection. We know how therapeutic it is for a psychologist to help us identify what we do not like about ourselves, not so much to fight it as to accept it as an integral part of our reality. The death of Narcissus allows for the birth of an adult, who is integrated, living in the truth of his or her being so that, when confronted by God, the individual discovers himself to be a sinner. Francis achieves the supreme goal of the ascetic path through perfect domination of himself, which implies accepting the miserable side in each one of us. The result of this pushes him to serve the most poor, to eat the same food as the leper and to "become the servant of the miserable ones,"[13] like a school for learning sanctity through the integration of what is lowest and most repugnant in life.

The following discourse by Francis is illustrative of his inclusion of the negative: "I know that you will never be a Friar Minor if you could not be in the situation that I am about to describe: being superior of the brothers, you go to the chapter room to, say, admonish the friars and, instead, they say to you: 'An illiterate and despicable man does not fit our company. So, we do not want you to rule over us, because you do not know how to speak, you are simple and an idiot.' In the end, you are ashamed in front of everyone, despised by all. I say to you, if you do not hear these words with the same affection, with the same inner joy, with the same desire to be holy, you will never be a Friar Minor."[14]

This paradox is continually present in the words and actions of Francis: on the one side the consciousness of his unique mission, and at the same time, the frailty of the one who carries out this mission. He held onto a sense of reality devoid of illusion about the fact of his being essentially "very poor, despised, and illiterate,"[15] as the bishop of Terni recognized when he compared Francis to the saints of the past who illuminated the Church with their wisdom and holiness. The Poverello went to him to say: "All men say that I am holy and they attribute to me the glory of holiness instead of attributing it to the Creator. You, on the other hand, a man of discernment, distinguish between what is vile and what is precious." Such an attitude was never meant to be an expression of humor, but of the consciousness of the other side of one and the same reality. Because of this, which grew even more, he could make the statement: "However, never be sure that I will never have sons and daughters. At any moment the Lord may take from me the treasure He has given me."[16]

What is even more curious, in all of this, is that the consciousness of the negative is never accompanied, as one might be led to believe, by a feeling of sadness and bitterness, but rather by happiness and profound joy. It is true that Francis wept in the forests to the point that everyone could hear his cries. The reason for his sadness, however, was not his own sinfulness, but rather the gentle mercy of God. He cried: "The Lord is not loved, the Lord is not loved." According to his way of thinking, it "is necessary to love with much love He that has loved us much." [17] The famous prayer of the *Absorbeat* ends marvelously: "That I may die for love of your love, you who were so good as to die for love of my love."

Joy That Includes the Negative

Joy, which is so characteristic of Franciscan spirituality, is born of a profound experience of the mercy of God; and mercy means the compassionate and gentle love of God, which is infinitely greater than all of our sins because He is greater than our heart; because of this, Jesus says in the Gospels, the merciful Father "loves the ungrateful and sinful" (Lk 6:35). [18] Francis was the most personal experience of that incommensurable mercy of God. Sins, as bad as they may be, can never hide the consolation that comes from this revelation: God loves us, in spite of our sins and even when we were His enemies. The concrete lesson that Francis derived from the experience of God the Father of our Lord Jesus Christ, Father of mercies and God of all consolations, is that sin accepted with humility and simplicity can also be a path toward the encounter with God. Not that sin ought to be sought after for itself; but sin should be understood as the expression of our decadent situation, that which is not totally involved in the mystery of redemption, sin that is wept for and lamented but without bitterness or debilitating desperation, because it will never be able to impede God from continuing to love and offering us forgiveness. The grace that is shown to us is always more abundant than the sin. It was a credit to Saint Francis always to be able to savor, joyfully, this excess of God revealed in his mercy.

Because God is Himself merciful with humanity and because Jesus was crucified—specifically, crucified because of his mercy—Francis wanted the relationships between the brothers to be characterized by an unlimited mercy. We have already commented upon a letter of the Fratello to a minister of the Friars Minor, two of the gentlest pages of Western spirituality. The minister was depressed because the brothers would not obey him, wanted to retire to a hermitage and consulted with the Seraphic Father. What shines through this counsel is radically human: "Love those who are proceeding in this way against you, not demanding anything of them that the Lord has not told you." [19]

As is readily seen, Francis never suggests a change in the others, but rather a change in the spirit of the minister. He refers to the typical attitude of the God of the New Testament, who is all-powerful in being able to support and love those who do good and evil (cf. Mt 5:45; Lk 6:35). Francis himself lived this kind of mercy even when he was minister general. He was aware that he could, if he wanted, rule over everyone,[20] but he opted to be, rather, "the least in the order." He understood that the task is "exclusively spiritual and consists in taming the vices and in correcting and healing them spiritually. Still, if they could not be corrected or healed with minor exhortations, observations, and examples, I never want to become a ruler who pushes and forces like a *podestá* of this world."[21] In other words, Francis wanted to go to the extreme of respecting the negativity of the others and so maintain a fraternity in spite of all the difficulties. To accept the shadows of the other means, in psychoanalytic language, to accept one's own shadows. The only way to conquer the diabolic is "in facing it honestly, integrating it within one's own system. . . . One becomes more 'human,' breaking all Pharisaism and breaking away from the habits of the human being who denies the demonic."[22]

The highest expression of this integration is found especially in the legend of perfect joy, already mentioned in connection with our discussion of liberation. It is a direct report by the historical Francis, as modern critics have ascertained.[23] In the lighthearted story of the *Fioretti*, it becomes clear that perfect joy does not reside in the positive, or more exactly, from the religious point of view, does not reside in what represents the possible, but rather in the negative accepted with love. Perfect joy or perfect liberty does not reside in being a famous saint, or in being an important miracle worker, or a burning charismatic, or a brilliant academician, or a missionary who converts all of the infidels to the Christian faith; but it does reside in accepting joyfully the rift in a fraternity, at being thrown out by the porter of that same community, recognizing as true that which is said to him, in the name of God: "You are two vagabonds who cheat the world and rob from the poor";[24] perfect joy or perfect liberty lies in welcoming, with pleasure, every kind of symbolic violence that demoralizes the interior convictions, and finally, in supporting with joy physical violence, "to be struck to the ground, throw in the snow and hit with a stick. . . ." The conclusion is clear: "Above all of the graces and all of the gifts of the Holy Spirit that Christ gives to his friends is that of conquering oneself and of freely out of love accepting work, injury, impropriety, and insult, because in all the other gifts of God [the positive] we cannot glory because they are not ours but God's . . . but in the cross of tribulation of each affliction we can glory in that this is indeed ourselves."[25]

In other words, perfect joy or perfect freedom results from a love so intense that we cannot support it, unless the negative is also loved and embraced joyfully. The one who interiorizes such a practice of love is the only one truly free, because nothing can threaten such a one: if he is raised to the heavens, his attitude is not changed by vanity, if he is thrown into the depths of hell, in the same way his attitude is not altered by bitterness. Such an individual possesses himself totally and so, no matter what the instance, it is neither good nor bad. The brilliance of such an achievement shines forth in permanent and unalterable joy. Francis, as seen in his biographies, had attained this freedom; thus, he is called "the ever-joyful brother."

A Great Temptation: The Tribute to Finitude

Human nature, as contemplated in the life of Francis, who achieved in his life the utopia of the Sermon on the Mount through his version of true joy, does not seem to belong to the contradictory pictures of this beautiful and tired century. Greek tragedy saw very plainly that when anyone tries to enter the arena of the divine and so enjoy a condition apart from mortal history, they are always struck down and reduced to that aspect of their nature that is finite. In Christian terms we would say: Francis could anticipate, extraordinarily, the anthropological eschatology by following and imitating *ecce homo* Jesus Christ; but he is not the new man, free from all of the pains of the history of sin. He never ceases to be a pilgrim and guest in the house of his true identity, despite the story of the condition of his sinful mortality and the promise of fullness that is subject to the eschatology of all times. As long as this does not occur, every individual and particularly the saint is subject to temptation.

In the last years of his life, Francis, as his intimate disciple Brother Leo assures us, passed through "a terrible spiritual temptation." The oldest account states: "He felt greatly disturbed, interiorly and exteriorly, in spirit and in body, to the point of avoiding contact with the other brothers, because of his not being able, owing to the temptation, to show his usual smile. He mortified himself by not eating and not speaking. He took refuge in the forest near the church of the Portiuncula in order to pray; there he could express his pain and shed many tears before the Lord, so that the Lord, for whom all is possible, might send from heaven some relief for his malady. For more than two years, day and night, he was tormented by this temptation."[26] This temptation overcame him at the time when he was obligated to write the definitive rule for the whole order, during 1221–23, in deeply changed conditions from those of the early humble community of Rivotorto. The number of Francis's followers was growing; he could no longer be with all of them personally to be the living *forma minorum;* many learned men had joined the movement; they opened many houses of studies, beginning with that of Saint Anthony in 1223 in Bologna, and then spreading throughout all of the provinces; the begging apostolate accepted by the friars made demands for formation and norms for work that would be somewhat continuous. The need for some rules was felt and yet Francis was a man of the spirit for whom one only needed to read the Gospel *sine glosse.*

The more scholarly and educated friars, through the mediation of Cardinal Hugolino, made Francis see that his evangelism and simplicity was not sufficient. There were already historically proven rules, like those of Saint Benedict, Saint Augustine, and Saint Bernard. Francis reacted strongly and tried to make him see that the Lord wanted a humble life and the path of simplicity and that Francis was a "new fool in the world."[27] It seemed to the brothers that these pressures were "a great sorrow and an even greater affliction"[28] for him. He became angry: "There are those friars who are opposed to me despite the fact that I am finally doing the will of God for the good and needs of the entire order!"[29] In 1220, recognizing that the order was escaping from his hands and that some other approach would be necessary, to meet the real demands of the great number of friars who supported organization and the spirit of the laws, he resigned from the office of minister general. He returned to do what he had started to do: serve the lepers and live with them.[30]

Inevitably, however, he continued to be the great inspiration he always was. Because of this, in 1221 he wrote a rule together with Brother Cesario de Espira, a biblical scholar; it was the *Regula non-bullata*, which preserves all the candor and newness of the Gospel spirit. But it did not grant any juridical assurance for a group that was forced to define itself concretely within a Church that controlled everything. They convinced Francis to write another. He went with Brother Leo and Brother Bonizzo, neither biblical scholars nor lawyers. This rule was not that different from the one written in 1221. The minister general, Brother Elias, after having submitted it for discussion, alleged that "it was lost because of carelessness."[31] Again, Francis had to go back to the splendid Rieti Valley, to Fonte Colombo, to try to write a new version.

It is then that there began Francis's great struggle to safeguard his dream of a fraternity based on radical poverty and on maternal service for one another, against the sensible friars, those conscious of human mediocrity and of those virtues possible to the majority of men, against men of his own order. A group of ministers provincial together with the minister general, Brother Elias, went to Francis and said to him: "These are the ministers who know you are composing a new rule, and knowing that it will most likely be too rigorous, they say that they will never accept it. What is easy for you is not easy for them!"[32] Francis, deeply distressed, turned his eyes toward heaven and said to Christ: "Lord, did I not tell you that they have no confidence in you? . . . I know how much human frailty can do and how much divine help is capable of. Those who do not want to observe the rule, let them leave the order!"[33]

Within this context, Francis sank into a dark night of the senses and spirit. He suffered illnesses that were apparent all over his body. He could never understand the reasoning of these others. Because of this, he found himself with contradictory feelings, the same as are found in a profound crisis or temptation, using religious terminology. On the one hand, he was capable of cursing, and on the other, of deep remorse. "Cursed may he be by you, most holy Lord, by the heavenly court and also by this little poor man because, by his poor example, he confuses and destroys that which you have built with the holy brothers of this order, a project that will never end."[34] Then he has compassion for those who, living in faithfulness, are called before the entire fraternity and made to live in the forests. At other times, as we have already mentioned above, he himself resigns from the post of minister general and is ashamedly thrown out of the fraternity; and he did so with joy, for to do otherwise would mean that he was not a brother or a Friar Minor.[35] Soon after, though, the original enthusiasm returns and he says: "Who are these who are trying to take the friars and the order from my hands? If I go to the general chapter, it will be to show them who I am."[36] Later, conscious of unwavering goodness and compassion for his adversaries, he says to himself: "I never want to be a despot like the *podestá* of this world."[37] In religious language (which by nature often deals with the transcendent), Francis externalizes the solutions as he finds them. He says to the Lord (in a devout reflection he is about to finish): "I am a poor and simple man. Tell me, why do you punish yourself so much when a friar leaves your order or when he does not follow the path you have pointed out to him? Tell me, who established the order of the friars? Was it not I?"[38]

Francis spent two years with these contradictory comings and goings. We do not know the details or the content of this terrible temptation. The texts we have looked at above reflect some clues of a painful and agonizing interior pilgrimage. It is true; because he was an individual who was sensitive to the things of the Spirit, he took everything seriously. There is also the rationality of his brother ministers, who argued from the logic of reasonability and common sense. Might they not be carriers of some message from God for him? Might his path of radicalness be truly insane, inappropriate for men who had the best of intentions, but were also loyal sons of the Church? Might he not have frustrated his companions in the beginning with his demented enthusiasm? Had he been terribly irresponsible in seducing the poor maidens of Clare's community with his insane love of God? Where should he go from here?

It was almost with the same desperation that, upon returning from the East in 1220–21, he went to the pope in Rome and asked for assistance in the person of a cardinal protector for the whole fraternity.[39] He was considerably relieved when in November of 1223 Pope Honorius III approved the actual rule, containing twelve chapters with minimal legal ordinances, agreed upon between Francis and the pope himself.

The integration of the problem that had brought on the temptation came to him while meditating in the chapel of the Portiuncula. He meditated upon faith, as tiny as a mustard seed, which could, nevertheless, move mountains. He understood that temptation is that mountain and that all he needed was a little faith. And this faith is gained by surrendering totally into the hands of God. At that very moment, according to the account, "the temptation vanished, he felt free and completely at peace."[40]

Therefore, Francis, in spite of all his difficulties, which are an integral part of our finitude, was faithful to his inner path: he integrated the negative with graciousness far beyond anything possible in terms of the pleasure principle or self-affirmation. That, in spite of the concessions, he was truly on the side of the ideal and not on the side of the brutality of history, on the side of Francis and not that of Elias, was shown by God Himself: He marked the body of Francis with the signs of failure that are the price of triumph, the stigmata of the Crucified One. The desire of Francis to be identified with Christ Crucified ended, by the work and grace of God, by his being also crucified. From now on there would be no more temptations of fidelity. He was given an inscription in flesh, letters that are accessible to all who, in faith, can read them: the stigmata, the sign of the truth of Jesus Christ.

To Live Joyfully with the Unchangeable

We do not live in the world we would like to, but rather in the world that has been imposed on us. We do not do everything we desire, but only that which we can and are allowed to do. Only an idealistic vision of history and of the individual conceives of liberty as pure spontaneity and creativity. Liberty is realized within a defined space, and the widening of that sphere always means an onerous process of liberation. It is a sign of maturity to accept calmly and with interior detachment those realities, objectively, we cannot change. Although, at times like these, we can exercise our freedom in the way that we accept and integrate within our own personal path the dictates of history. For this we need, as the ancient Greeks said, *amor fati*, love of the inevitable, embraced without bitterness but also without servility. This is what Francis did with respect to the impositions of the Church and of the ministers of the order (*praelati*), and with respect to the future of his charism.

In the *Legend of Perugia*, behind which is the intimate friend of

Francis, Brother Leo, we read: "We, those who were at his side while he composed the rule and almost all of his writings, are witnesses that that rule, like these writings, included many things that some, above all the superiors (*praelati*), were against . . . but because he was an enemy of all scandal, he condescended, much to his regret, to the wishes of the brothers.[41]

Through critical historical studies,[42] we know that many important points of the definitive rule had to be accepted by Francis because of the counsel and insistence of the brother ministers, of the Roman Curia, or of the pope himself. So, for example, at the beginning of the rule, where he speaks of observing the Holy Gospel, the added "in obedience, without property and in chastity" comes from the Roman Curia, since Innocent III already was concerned with the juridical definition of the new lay movements. The original intent of Francis of a living of the Gospel open to the world and among the poor is contained here and leveled within the parameters of a spirituality of religious vows; the lay character gives way to the religious character.

The omission of the texts that allowed him to define his evangelical vocation (Mt 10:9; Lk 9:3; 10:4) must have been especially painful for Francis: "Do not carry anything for your journey, neither purse, nor knapsack, nor bread, nor money, nor staff, and do not resist those who mistreat you." In this way, the brothers ceased to be poor pilgrims, as Francis wanted them to be.[43]

In the same way, the correction of guilty brothers was profoundly modified. In the *Regula non-bullata* and in the *Letter to a Minister*, Francis desires an unlimited mercy in the context of an affectionate fraternal life; in the definitive rule the context is discipline, demanding that the ministers be granted the canonical recourse reserved for grave sins.

In the same way, through the intervention of Cardinal Hugolino or the Roman Curia, the article was abolished that referred to the great spiritual liberty and the right of resistance that allowed the brothers to disobey the ministers "when they are asked to do something contrary to our way of life and contrary to the soul." If one felt it impossible to observe the rule purely and simply, he could go to his minister; and the minister had to help him find a solution, as he would want to be helped if he were in a similar situation. Francis wanted to guarantee to each one the right to fidelity to his own vocation. All of this disappears in the definitive rule.

With the growth of the order and the involvement of the brothers in ministry, some original intentions had to be modified. So, the definitive rule does not impose manual labor for all with the same rigor as before, nor does it prohibit them from having books, when in the third chapter of the *Regula non-bullata* it says that the brothers must have "more books than necessary to pray the Divine Office."

We know that Francis considered the Gospel fraternity in perfect equality as a way of living the mystery of the Church as a privileged place for the activity of the Holy Spirit, true minister general of the order. He wanted to include in the rule the following words: "In God there is no distinction between persons, and the minister general of the order, who is the Holy Spirit, descends in the same way on the poor as on the rich." Celano tells us that these words could not be included in the *Regula bullata*.[44]

Having to fit within the greater realities of the Church, and even those of history with its demands, certainly made Francis suffer; but no negative attitude, as if he had not accepted that reality, can be observed in him. The external determination can be an occasion for internal growth and the opportunity to be respectful and solidary with differences. Francis became stronger accepting such determinations.[45]

Welcome, Sister Death

When life is turned around, we find ourselves inevitably together with death. One of the most difficult traumas to resolve for the human psyche and for the attainment of freedom is exactly that of death. It seems like the supreme negation of life. It frustrates the most fundamental driving force of the life system, according to Freud, the true dynamic nucleus of each being, that is, desire.[46] Desire is radically the desire for life without any negation, desire for an always real freedom and for a limitless happiness. In other words, the dynamic of life calls to life, invites one to live forever. Not without reason is it said that the structure of desire is omnipotence, because not only is this or that thing desired, but it is desired in its fullness, totally. Tradition calls this drive for life Eros.

As such, this omnipotence is realized only within the sphere of desire; in the sphere of reality it is constantly denied. There are frustrations and denials that oblige desire to accept and that open the door of possibilities. The experience of death is given as a limitation of life and of the meaning of reality. It is the presence of Thanatos, of death. Life and death, desire and reality, develop a dialectical drama, forming the tapestry of human life.

In fact, human life is an uninterrupted series of realizations of frustrated desire, learning to deny, obliged to accept, and forced to overcome. We ask ourselves: Is a synthesis possible that would not be the recovery of the former, but rather the achievement of a level of human unity, higher and more lasting? A question like that is also the fruit of desire. And it is then that the specter of death appears, like a person who devours all and who, indifferent to all human destiny, equalizes everything. A sign of human and religious maturity is to integrate the trauma of death in the context of life. Then death is dethroned from its status as lord of life and ultimate reality. Eros triumphs over Thanatos and desire wins the game. But there is a price to pay for this immortality: the acceptance of the mortality of life. The acceptance of death, the frustrating of empirical and superficial desire that demands eternal life, is the condition by which desire achieves its truth of living forever, in absolute triumph. We find this process of the acceptance of death in a marvelous manner in the life of Saint Francis.[47] It is not often that we find someone accepting death to the point of greeting it as a much-loved sister and dying while singing, as Thomas of Celano tells us Francis did.

It was the year 1226. Francis was tremendously weak. The illness of his stomach had advanced so much that Brother Leo recounts that he began to vomit blood.[48] The sores on his legs also reached his stomach and he could no longer retain any food. Celano comments: "The doctors were frightened and the brothers marveled that his spirit could live in a body already so destroyed, because his flesh had been consumed, and there only remained the skin on his bones."[49]

From Siena they moved him to Assisi. Through the streets and villages he exhorted the curious, who came in great numbers, to bear the cross of Christ. To the brothers, however, he exhorted: "Let us begin to serve the Lord, because until now we have done little."[50] In Assisi, they took him to the bishop's palace. When a doctor from Arezzo attended him and determined that nothing could be done except wait for death, Francis exclaimed with indescribable joy: "Welcome, Sister Death." He called to the Brothers Angelo and Leo so that they might sing the "Canticle of Brother Sun." Then he added a verse to the canticle: "Praised may you be, my Lord, for Sister Bodily Death, whom no one escapes. Woe to those who die in mortal sin! Blessed be those who fulfill the will of God, because the second death will do them no harm." And the biographers relate that the brothers sang often during the day to encourage the spirit of Francis, who was almost dead, and during the night to cheer and edify the guardians of the palace.[51]

Such joviality was a scandal to common sense. The general of the order, Brother Elias, seeing the uselessness of the situation, said to Francis: "Father, I am very glad that you feel so much joy; but I fear that in the city, where they take you for a saint, it would be scandalous for them to see that you are not preparing properly for a good death." "Do not be troubled," Francis answered him. "With all my sufferings I feel so close to God that I can do nothing but sing."[52] He is faithful to the end of his original path, the path of a fool,[53] fool for the Gospel and for the following of the Crucified Lord.

Sensing that his last hour was fast approaching, Francis made known his desire to die where everything had started, the Chapel of Our Lady of the Angels of the Portiuncula. The magistrates of Assisi organized an entire armed guard to accompany him. From the height of the city, crossing rocky and woody paths, they made their way to the Portiuncula. Close to the leprosarium, he asked that they place him on the ground facing the city of Assisi. From that place could be seen the white city, perched on the cliff of the mountain, with its towers and walls; to the right could be seen the monastery of San Damiano, and in the background Mount Subasio. He remained in silence for a long time, contemplating that familiar landscape, which his eyes could no longer see, but which still shone in his interior world. Then, raising his hand with difficulty, he blessed the city with these memorable words: "May the Lord bless you, my beloved city. In the past you were the stronghold of highwaymen; now God has chosen you as the home for those who know Him and who breathe the perfume of holy life. I beg you, my Lord Jesus Christ, father of mercies, not to forget the abundance of graces with which you have blessed her, that she may always be a home for those who glorify your blessed name, forever and ever. Amen."[54]

At Saint Mary of the Angels they placed him in a cell very close to the chapel. His spirit was awake; he asked the brothers to continue singing and he himself intoned, as best he could, the song of David: "In a loud voice I cried to the Lord, with all my voice I cry out."[55] Then a series of deeply sacramental gestures took place, whose secret only Francis himself knew, in which primitive archetypes of integration and identification with all things took place. In the first place, Francis exteriorized a feeling of radical reconciliation: "My child, God calls me. To my brothers, those here as well as those absent, I pardon them of all offenses and guilt, and as much as I am able, I absolve them; when you tell them these things, bless them in my name."[56] Then he asked the brothers to place him naked on the earthen floor, to "fight nakedly with the naked one."[57] It was a gesture that rose from his innermost being. More than an extreme identification with the naked Crucified Lord, it expressed the profound desire of the psyche for communion with Mother Earth;[58] we come naked from her and we return to her naked. Like an immense uterus, she thrusts us from her embracing womb, representing thusly, and in the language of symbols, the total integration of humanity with God, the great and good Mother. Francis was conscious that this gesture expressed the highest moment of his path toward his Father. Because of this he said to the brothers: "I have completed my task. May Christ teach you to complete yours."[59]

Then he said goodbye to all the brothers; he blessed them, imposing his hands. He made his last recommendations, making it clear that "the holy Gospel is more important than all the rules."[60] Goodbye, "all my children, remain always in the fear of the Lord and remain always in Him."[61]

He did not forget his beloved sister Clare. Knowing that she was crying uncontrollably, he sent her the following message: "I, poor Brother Francis, desire to follow until the end the poverty of our Lord Jesus Christ and of his Most Holy Mother; I beg you, my sisters, that you never stray from this path, although in the future they will suggest something else to you." And he said to the messenger: "Go and tell Lady Clare to cease all sadness and pain because she cannot see me now; may she know that she and her sisters will see me and will have great consolation in this."[62] Nor did he forget Jacoba, a rich Roman widow who was a great friend of Francis: "Without a doubt, she would be very sad if she knew that I left this world without having told her beforehand." He dictated the following letter for her: "To the Lady Jacoba, servant of God, Brother Francis, the little poor one of Christ, health in the Lord and union in the Holy Spirit. Most beloved friend, I have to tell you that the end of my life approaches; thus has the blessed Christ himself shown me. Because of this, if you still wish to see me alive, come right away. Bring a strip of cloth to wrap my body, and everything needed for the burial. I ask you also to bring those delicious cookies that you prepared for me when I was ill in Rome. . . ." He was still dictating the letter when Jacoba arrived. A brother ran to Francis's bed and told him: "I bring you good news." These words were enough for Francis to understand, and he exclaimed: "Blessed be God. Open the door, because for Sister Jacoba there is no cloister." And she stayed there until the joyful passing (*transitus*) of Francis.[63]

Finally, Francis's intuitive soul still realized a gesture of great sacramental meaning. He did the same thing as Jesus, on his last night, demonstrating in this way all the love that he had for his brothers."[64] He took bread, blessed it, broke it, and gave it to those present. He also commanded that the Gospel of Saint John be read, beginning with the passage: "Before the feast of Passover . . ." (Jn 13:1ff.). Francis was no more than a deacon; he did not intend to assume the power of consecration, but he wanted to imitate Jesus to the end. And so, he realized the celebration of the new and eternal covenant.

All the biographers write that, in the grip of death, "he invited all creatures to praise the Lord . . . and even death itself, which all fear and dread." Realizing that the moment of his parting was already near, with great courtesy and in the spirit of hospitality so characteristic of his way of life, he said: "Welcome, Sister Death." He encouraged the doctor who was treating him by saying: "Brother Doctor, do not be afraid of telling me of the closeness of death. It is for me the door to life."[65]

Finally, he asked that they again place him naked on the ground, and in honor of his funereal and friendly guest, he sprinkled ashes on his body. Then, with a very weak voice, he chanted Psalm 142: *Voce mea ad Dominum clamavi* (with my voice I called to the Lord). Coming to the verse *educ de custodia animam meam* (take my soul from its prison, that it may sing your name, for the just await me, and You mete out the reward), he became profoundly silent. He died singing.

The legend says that, in this twilight moment, hundreds of larks flew over Francis's cell, sadly lamenting with their song the death of their brother. This same legend adds: "The brothers saw the soul of their most holy father like a star as big as the moon and as brilliant as the sun, rising upon a white cloud toward heaven."[66] The legends keep the truth of empirical fact hidden.

This way of assimilating the trauma of death, transforming it into a supreme expression of liberty, and as such, of humanization, poses a series of questions. What way of life did Francis live to assimilate in this way within the very plan of life the sinister character of death? What does death and the process of dying mean in a life thus described? We will attempt to probe these questions in light of the path of Francis toward death.

Death Belongs to Life

Francis sings to death, but he does not do so as a romantic *avant la lettre* who sings morbidly to approaching death. His perception is realistic: "No man can escape death." Beyond this statement is the consciousness of the tragedy that hangs over human destiny, over its realizations, its aspirations, its holiness, and that has its origin in the principle of desire. Death devours everything, This death, which seems tragic, is sung by Francis as a beloved sister. How can that which devours all life be considered a sister, to which almost no one opens the door but rather receives it weeping uncontrollably?

It seems to us that there appears in the life of Francis two dimensions that shed light on his reconciliation with death: the acceptance of the mortality of life and his identification with the Source of life.

Francis's course consists of a gradual, and finally, perfect integration of the fundamental conflict of life: the conflict between desire and reality, between life instincts (Eros) and death instincts

(Thanatos), between flesh and spirit, between uranic impulses (upward) and telluric impulses (downward). He achieved, by the work and grace of mystery, the acceptance of life as it is, in its demand for eternity, but also in its mortality. Life, because of the structure of creation, is mortal, because God wished it so, Death, in a correct existential understanding, is not made manifest only at the end of life, as the ultimate instance of human existence. It is already present from the beginning in the proper essence of life. When we are born, we begin to die and we continue to die throughout life, until we end by dying. Death belongs, then, to life. This situation of mortality does not arise because of sin. It is this way because God made life mortal. In the dawn of his condition, Adam (humanity) was destined to die because the proper structure of earthly life, in time and space, is articulated by a fragile balance that is slowly disintegrated until completely diluted. But humanity accepted death as something normal and desired by God, just as it accepted birth or waking from a dream. Death did not threaten life, but this type of life, mundane and mortal, opens the door to another type of life, eternal and immortal, in God. Within the mortality of life, humanity would walk toward eternal life, creating throughout its course of freedom a personal form of this eternal life.[67]

Sin dramatized the acceptance of death as belonging to life and to the mystery of the good creation of God. Sin introduced the closing off of understanding, shutting off the vision of the structure of mortal life, making enemies of life and death. Death is seen only as the total negation of life. Because of this, humanity held on to life, as it could thus escape death. But this is fatal and cruel. From there, the gap between death and life begins to form; fear of death blossoms and desperation rises at the first hint of its proximity.

This way of seeing death is something unpleasant and a consequence of sin. Because of this, Saint Paul says correctly that with sin death entered the world (cf. Rom 5:12; 1 Cor 15:21–22; Gn 2:17; Wis 2:23ff.; Eccl 25:33), that is, this real death, just as it is feared and experienced by all. The Christian plan of conversion as a recovery of lost humanity means the achievement of naturalness before death, embracing it as a necessary condition for the encounter with the Life of God.

Francis is seen as the dawning Adam: he lived the perspective of the Gospel so radically that he made it possible for original innocence to emerge in him. Death appears, then, in its vital character, ceasing to be the enemy of life *tout court*, and appears as a step from this type of life to another and definitive way of life in God, immortal and complete. In this perspective, Francis could accept everything as coming from God. He integrated everything in a vital unity, courteously accepting even death, which became for him a companion in life, a sister on the voyage.

What does it mean to accept death within life? It means to accept the hints of death, like, for example, limitations, illnesses, ignorance, corporal and spiritual weakness, and all infirmities. As a consequence, Francis was deeply tolerant of human smallnesses, his own as well as those of others. In his major legend, Saint Bonaventure recounts: "Francis suffered every type of infirmity, so painful that none of his limbs was free of atrocious suffering. He ended not having anything but skin and bones. But these very infirmities were not enemies for him but sisters; he supported them with patience and joy and gave thanks to God for them." [68] He accepted, then, mortality, not with bitterness but with joy, like one who finds in it the truth of one's own life. Just as he always accepted the mortality of life, he also accepted joyfully the ultimate step of life, death.

Identification with the Source of Life

The proof of the acceptance of death as pertaining simply to life reveals the spiritual and religious greatness of Francis. But this is not enough to understand the proper way for Francis to relate with death. A calm stoic and a cold rationalist can also face this sinister situation of life with honor and self-control. A shining example of this was Freud, father of modern psychology. A cancer of the face made life intolerable for him. "His bed had to be covered with mosquito netting because the fetid odor that emanated attracted the flies. . . . He suffered terribly and nights were a torture . . . but none of this lessened his constant cordiality. Not even once during his illness, says his best biographer, Max Schuler, could one see in him any sign of impatience or rejection or anger toward any of the people who visited him." [69] He died serenely, accepting, faithful to his own theory, the principle of reality and the imperative of death.

In the case of Francis, things are different. He dies greeting death amiably; he dies singing, beyond all stoicism and resignation in the face of the inevitable principle of mortal reality. Only one who is already beyond death itself, or who has incorporated it in his or her own life, can greet and sing to death. Nor should one think that there is in Francis the reserve of hope that comes to us because of the certainty of the resurrection of Christ, a guarantee of our own resurrection. There is not one single reference with respect to this in the first biographies. The joy of the Poverello springs from a deeper source. His link with life, nature, all people was so radical that it reached the root of that which gives life to all, reaching that Source from which comes all that exists and all that moves—God.

Between Francis and God there were ties of such great intimacy that Francis felt, "as much as God is God, as much as He is the Living and the Source of all life, I will not die, though I may physically die." The overcoming of the tragic character of death springs from the certainty and the radicalness of loving and feeling loved. The Christian philosopher Gabriel Marcel refers in this way to this experience: "If you love me, I know it, I will never die." How much greater is this true in Francis, with his refined and extremely sensitive soul to all that is from God, feeling loved by God to the very depths of his being? And according to what we believe, this is the reason for his joy in the face of death. Whoever drinks, as he drank, from the fountain of life cannot die, though he or she may have to pass through the terrible night of the senses and of the spirit. From an enemy, death becomes a sister. She is the necessary *transitus* toward a new and definitive birth. It can be painful, as is every birth, but it makes possible a new advent of life, now full in God.

No one can escape death, as Francis understood very well. And because of this, we all live to die. But this is not a tragedy, because we die to rise again. Death appears, thus, like a holy drama. It happens as in all plays, and not in tragedies, that everything ends well and with great promise. Because it is this way, he can truly sing to death: "Welcome, Sister Death." With this attitude, death discovers its true face: the face of a friend and sister.

Those who come to integrate in a complete way the negative, and especially the trauma of death, certainly achieve the kingdom of freedom. Nothing will threaten them anymore, because they no longer have enemies. The kingdom of liberty means, then, the Kingdom of God. The Kingdom of God is the concretization of the supreme utopia, of God who dies with those who love Him, and who "will dry the tears from their eyes and there will be no more death, nor cries, nor pain, because all that was will be no more" (Ap 21:4). Francis anticipated this utopia and demonstrated its truth.

Conclusion

SAINT FRANCIS: A HUMANISTIC
AND CHRISTIAN ALTERNATIVE

C ontact with Francis produces a very profound and welcome
crisis. His image is for us a shining halo, which reveals to
us our mediocrity and slowness in the face of the calls that
come to us from the deepest truths of the heart and of the Gospel.
He oriented his life within the utopia, and kept it alive like a coal
among the ashes of all the routines and rationality of history. He
incorporated the archetype of integration of the most distant links;
he historicized the myth of the reconciliation of heaven and earth,
of abyss and mountain. It is there that the fascination arises, and
human and religious catharsis operate.

Before Francis of Assisi, we discover ourselves as imperfect and
old. He seems to us to be something new and something of the
future we are all searching for, although he was born eight hundred
years ago. But this feeling does not cause bitterness, because his
message contains so much sweetness that the mediocre feel pushed
to be good, the good to be perfect, and the perfect to be holy. No
one is left indifferent to his strong and gentle call.

With his attitudes, Francis places us immediately before the Gospel and the Sermon on the Mount. He took the message of Jesus
absolutely seriously, as if it were personally directed toward him.
He accepted it in its totality, *ad litteram et sine glossa,* and he forced
himself to live it with a generous and joyful heart. He did not want
to know anything of interpretations. He knew very well that for
the most part the interpretations are nothing but a castration of

the strength of the Gospel, and the Gospel was, simply, for him, his *formula vitae*.

If he always tried to direct his life from the Gospel and not from the sensibility of rationality, he was not, however, a fanatic. Because of this he embraced the Gospel life; he also demonstrated the sense of a rule; if he lived from charism, he also understood the institution; if he submitted himself to hard penances, he also knew how to be happy and to be courteous with everyone; if he accepted radical poverty, he also postulated an extremely sensible fraternity, sensitive to the meeting of the needs of each one; if he was rigorous with himself, he was at the same time compassionate with the brother who cried out at night: "I am dying of hunger."

He always referred to two poles, but holding on, primarily and firmly, to the pole of the Gospel. He fearlessly broke down the irreplaceable walls, to insure Gospel liberty. Because of this, strength and gentleness coexisted in him, which resulted from the constant tension between the Gospel and the rule, between the Sermon on the Mount and the order. If there had only been strength, he would have been a hard saint, inflexible and heartless. If there had only been gentleness, he would have projected the image of a sentimental saint, sweet and formless. Gentleness and strength coexist in one and the same person, making the sun of Assisi shine, as Dante would say, a sun generating at the same time, light and heat, the sun sung by the Poverello, as "beautiful, shining, and of great splendor," but also the moon with its pleasant and serene light that calms all the arrows that harm and draw blood. Francis shines in this way like a solar and lunar man, a happy integration of opposites. Francis also represents a call of singular importance for our present-day situation. We live in a world of things; everything is an object of change, of interest, of negotiation, of falsification, of disguise and fetish. More and more, things lose their direct human use for the satisfaction of objective necessities that must be attended to collectively. With his radical poverty, Francis postulates a radical disappropriation, especially of money, whose nature resides in being a pure object of change with no other use than as change. He begins, in the exact moment of the birth of the capitalistic spirit, supported by interchange, a human existence that is based only on the value of use: two tunics, a capuche, shoes for those who need them, and tools for prayer and work. The absence of any rule is meant to leave the path free of all obstacles for the encounter of human beings in their transparency as brothers, serving each other, as is fitting to the members of one family. This endeavor may appear utopian, and in fact it is. But, utopia belongs to reality, because it does not reside in that which is or can be measured, but much more in that which is possible and which may be in the future. Utopia expresses all the possibilities of reality in their concrete form. Because, although they may not become real, they bring forth new realizations, to overcome that which is already accomplished and learned in order to achieve fuller and more humanizing forms. Francis's utopia of a fraternity of equal values, and as such nonexploitative, encourages the modern social and personal cost possible.

The Gospel seriousness of Francis is surrounded by lightheartedness and enchantment because it is profoundly imbued with joy, refinement, courtesy, and humor. There is in him an invincible confidence in humanity and in the merciful goodness of the Father. As a result, he exorcises all fears and threats. His faith does not alienate him from the world; nor does it lead him into a pure valley of tears. On the contrary, it transforms him through gentleness and care in land and home for the fraternal encounter, where persons do not appear as "children of necessity, but as children of joy" (Gaston Bachelard). We can dance in the world because it is the theater of the glory of God and of his children.

Francis of Assisi, more than an idea, is a spirit and a way of life. The spirit and way of life are only made manifest in practice, not in a formula, idea, or ideal. Everything in Francis invites practice: *exire de saeculo*, leaving the imperial system, in an alternative act that makes real more devotion toward others, more gentleness with the poor, and greater respect for nature.

Notes

LIST OF ABBREVIATIONS

All references to Franciscan sources may be found in *St. Francis of Assisi: Omnibus of Sources* (Chicago, 1973).

Adm	Admonitions of St. Francis
1Cel	Celano's *First Life of St. Francis*
2Cel	Celano's *Second Life of St. Francis*
3Cel	Celano's *Treatise of the Miracles*
Fior	*Fioretti* or Little Flowers of St. Francis
LetF	Letter to All the Faithful
LetCle	Letter to All Clerics
LetMin	Letter to a Minister
LetSup	Letter to All Superiors of the Friars Minor
LetRul	Letter to the Rulers of the People
LetLeo	Letter to Brother Leo
LetAnth	Letter to Saint Anthony
LetO	Letter to a General Chapter
LM	*Major Life of St. Francis* by St. Bonaventure
Lm	*Minor Life of St. Francis* by St. Bonaventure
LP	Legend of Perugia
MP	Mirror of Perfection
1R	*First Rule* of St. Francis
2R	*Second Rule* of St. Francis
SalVir	Salutation of the Blessed Virgin Mary
TC	Legend of the Three Companions
Test	Testament of St. Francis

Chapter 1—Saint Francis: Model of Gentleness and Care

1. For a succinct background, see R. Barthes, R. Dumont, M. Duverger, and others, *Quelle crise? Quelle société?* (Grenoble, 1974).

2. The bibliography is immense; we cite the most representative names that work

on the problem with particular acuity: on the level of psychoanalysis, the works of Rollo May and Erich Fromm; of industrial society, Herbert Marcuse and T. Horkheimer; of philosophy, M. Heidegger, J. Ladrière, and P. Ricoeur; of theology, the liberation theologians R. Alves, G. Gutiérrez, and L. Boff.

3. See the following texts that serve as a good orientation: P. Mantoux, *The Industrial Revolution in the Eighteenth Century* (London, 1971); E. J. Hobsbawn, *The Age of Revolution: Europe 1789–1848* (London, 1962); id., *Industry and Empire* (Baltimore, 1969).

4. See the masterly balance of the destinies of rationality in J. Ladrière, *Les enjeux de la rationalité: Le défi de la science et de la technologie aux cultures* (Paris, 1977). We refer here to the fact that the meaning of the Greek Logos, just as the Cartesian Cogito did not have, in the original, a reductive meaning. But there was an accent that ended by underscoring the other nuances and that dominated previous history. The full sense of Logos and Cogito continued in the underground of our culture and in this way was always present.

5. Rollo May, *Eros e Repressão* (Petropolis, 1973), p. 108 [*Love and Will* (New York, 1969)].

6. Rollo May dedicates an entire book to this problem, *Power and Innocence* (New York, 1972), esp. pp. 40–54: "Innocence and the End of an Era."

7. On the level of the Church, this problematic became particularly perceptible in the magisterium of Pope Paul VI, speaking of the proper form of faith (less analytic) of the "civilization of love." There are strong repercussions in the Puebla document, nos. 1188ff. Message to the peoples of Latin America, no. 8.

8. Rollo May, *Power and Innocence*, p. 204; see also pp. 93–98, 202–6.

9. "Le destin de la raison et les taches de la philosophie," in *Vie sociale et Destinée* (Gembloux, 1973), p. 35.

10. For a theory of affectivity as a basis for the reflections of Heidegger and of Henry, see J. Ladrière, *Vie sociale et Destinée*, pp. 149–55.

11. Fragment 282 of the *Pensées;* cf. the commentary by R. Guardini, *Pascal* (Morcelliana, 1956), pp. 150ff., and M. F. Sciacca, *Pascal* (Milan, 1972), pp. 138–48, 199–203.

12. For Plato, Eros is the central energy that drives the spirit, pushing it relentlessly toward the beautiful, the true, the just, and the good. Eros "wants to possess the Good eternally" (*Banquet*, 203d). The investigations of A. Nygren are classic: *Eros und Agape: Gestaltwandlung der christlichen Liebe* (Gütersloh, 1930); H. Scholz, *Eros und Caritas: Die platonische Liebe und die Liebe im Sinn des Christentums* (Halle, 1929); E. Fuchs, *Le désir et la tendresse* (Geneva, 1980).

13. *Love and Will*, p. 80.

14. G. Hultgren, *Le commandement d'amour chez Augustin* (Paris, 1939), esp. the last chapter. The phrase of Pascal is well-known: "It is the heart that knows God and not reason" (*Pensées*, no. 278); as well as the other fragment (277): "This is what faith is: God sensed by the heart and not by reason." Note that Pascal does not speak of knowing God, but sensing God, that knowledge that leads to union with Him.

15. *Eros e Civilização*, p. 118.

16. The word *enthusiasm* is much richer and belongs to the phenomenon that we are analyzing, because, etymologically, it means the presence of the Divine within existence: en-*theos*-mos.

17. *Sein und Zeit*, pt. I, chap. 6, pp. 41 and 42.

18. The myth of Care goes like this: "One day, Care, crossing a river, saw a bit of clay. Carefully he began to mold a human figure. And as he reflected upon what he had done, Jupiter appeared, the god of the sky. Care asked him to breathe spirit into the human and Jupiter accepted gladly. But when Care wanted to give his own name to the creature he had molded, Jupiter forbade it, demanding that his name be given. While the two were arguing, Earth stood up and manifested the desire of giving her name to the creature that had been molded by Care, because it had been

formed from part of her body. They then asked Saturn (god of time) to be the referee. He made the following decision that seemed right to all concerned: Because you, Jupiter, gave it spirit, you will receive this spirit at the hour of death; and because you, Earth, gave it body, you will receive it after death. But because Care was the one who molded the creature, it will remain in his power while it lives. And because you were arguing about what name to give it, I want it to be called Homo, that is, made from the humus of the earth." See the commentaries by Rollo May of this myth and its variations in *Eros and Repressão*, pp. 322–36.

19. *Pensées*, p. 125.

20. Cf. J. Ladrière, *Os desafios da Racionalidade* (Petropolis, 1979), p. 209.

21. *La convivialità* (Mondadori, 1974), esp. pp. 31ff., 48–53 [*Tools for Conviviality* (New York, 1973)].

22. Luís Inacio da Silva (Lula), *Lula sem Censura* (Petropolis, 1981).

23. Rollo May, *Power and Innocence*, p. 41.

24. M. Scheler, *Wesen und Formen der Sympathie* (Bonn 1926), p. 110.

25. *Paradiso*, cant. XI, 50.

26. See the excellent reflections of A. Conti, *San Francesco* (Florence, 1931), pp. 169–73; R. Schneider, *Die Stunde des hl. Franziskus von Assisi* (Heidelberg, 1946), 100–101.

27. Following this line of thought, see F. Duhourcau, *Le saint des temps de misère, François d'Assise* (Paris, 1936), pp. 379–81; Herman Hesse, *Franz von Assisi* (Berlin and Leipzig, 1904), pp. 8–9: "Francis united heaven and earth in his heart and ignited with the ember of eternal life the earthly and mortal world."

28. Sigmund Freud, *O Mal-estar na Cultura* (Rio de Janeiro, 1963) [*Civilization and Its Discontents* (New York, 1962)].

29. *Politics* II, 7, 1267b, 3–5.

30. See the very good study by C. Surian, *Elementi per una teologia del desiderio e la spiritualità di San Francesco d'Assisi* (Rome, 1973), pp. 188–91: "Francesco, uomo di desiderio."

31. Saint Bonaventure, LM 14,1: at the end of his life he said: "Let us begin, brothers, to serve the Lord for up till now we have done nothing."

32. LM 4,12.

33. LM 12,2; 1Cel 91.

34. LM 3,1; TC 25; 1Cel 22.

35. 1Cel 71; 98.

36. In the writings of Saint Francis, the predominance of "doing" over "understanding" is visibly noted, of heart over reason, of love over truth. "Doing" appears 170 times as opposed to 5 of "understanding" (of which two are biblical citations); "heart" appears 42 times as opposed to 1 of "intelligence" (citing Mk 12:33); "love" appears 23 times as opposed to 12 of "truth"; "mercy" is cited 26 times while "intellect" is cited only once. Cf. I. Boccali, *Concordantiae verbales opusculorum S. Francisci et S. Clarae Assisiensium* (Assisi, 1976). The *Legend of the Three Companions*, 57, says very well: "Whatever he said in word, he showed in his deeds with affection and solicitude."

37. LP 74.

38. LM 9,6; 1Cel 56.

39. Someone once asked him how he put up with the cold in winter with such miserable clothing, and he responded: "It would be easy for us to put up with this external cold if within we were burning with the desire for our celestial homeland" (LM 5,1).

40. LM 5,1; cf. 1Cel 40: the difficult penances of the first companions.

41. See the work of the two great Franciscan scholars completely centered in this perspective: Cajetan Esser and E. Grau, *Respuesta al Amor* (Santiago de Chile, CEFEPAL, 1981) [*Love's Reply* (Chicago, 1963)], and Ch. Dukker, *Umkehr des Herzens* (Werl/West, 1956).

42. 2Cel 211.

43. LM 5,7. The Legend of Perugia begins this way, according to the edition of Delorme: "From the austerity of the saint with himself and from the discrete softness with others" (LP 50).

44. LM 5,7; 2Cel 22; LP 1; MP 27. With another brother he ate some grapes early in the morning (LP 5). He was also indulgent with himself; in his illness he asked for fish, to drink wine, to hear music and the sweets of brother Jacoba de Settesoli (LM 5,10; LP 29; MP 28).

45. 2Cel 129.

46. 2Cel 211; cf. LP 96.

47. 2Cel 211.

48. *Chronicle of Jordan of Giano*, 17.

49. 2Cel 191.

50. LP 90.

51. Cf. 1Cel 2: "He was very humane, gentle and affable"; 17: "He also favored, still living in the times and following its maxims, other poor people, stretching out his generous hand to those who had nothing, and to the afflicted he extended the affection of his heart . . ."; 83: "How enchanting he was . . . in fraternal charity, in emotional relationships . . . very proper when he gave counsel, always faithful to his obligations."

52. 1Cel 83.

53. LM 1,1; 2Cel 8.

54. 2Cel 8.

55. Id. 83, 175.

56. 1Cel 75; see the appropriate reflections of K. Beyschlag, *Die Bergpredigt und Franz von Assisi* (Gütersloh, 1955), pp. 189–200: "The Problem of Mercy in Francis."

57. Testament 1.

58. 1Cel 17; 2Cel 9.

59. MP 44.

60. 1Cel 103.

61. 2Cel 85; see how he punished himself when he thought he had offended a poor man in MP 58.

62. See the detailed study of F. Uribe Escobar, *Struttura e specificità della vita religiosa secondo la regola e gli opusculi di S. Francesco d'Assisi* (Rome, 1979), pp. 314–22.

63. This idea is very present in the Franciscan texts: LetLeo; Adm 6; MP 43; 1Cel 84; 115; 2Cel 17; 216; *Chronicle of Jordan de Giano*, 2.

64. The best is that of H. Grundmann, *Religiöse Bewegungen im Mittelalter* (Hildesheim, 1961).

65. 2Cel 217; LP 117; MP 68; LM 14,4.

66. See my comparative study of the experience of Jesus and that of Francis: "Jesus de Nazaré e Francisco de Assis," in *Nosso Irmao Francisco de Assis* (Petropolis, 1975), pp. 111–35. Cf. 1Cel 84: "His supreme aspiration, his most living desire and his highest purpose was to observe in everything and always the holy Gospel and to follow the teachings of our Lord Jesus Christ and his footsteps with utmost attention, with every care, with all the desire of his mind, with all the fervor of his heart."

67. See the various prayers in the short works, primarily chapter 23 of the *Regula non-bullata*.

68. Cf. 2Cel 85.

69. MP 93; cf. 1Cel 84: "He had so present in his thoughts the humility of the incarnation and the charity of the passion that he had difficulty thinking of anything else."

70. 2CtaF 56.

71. 2Cel 199.

72. 1Cel 84.

73. 2Cel 199–200. Francis had a deep devotion for the Eucharist. The insignifi-

cance of the material elements, bread and wine, prolonged for him the humility of the mystery of the Incarnation. "His love for the sacrament of the body of the Lord was a fire that warmed his entire being, leaving him in a deep stupor when contemplating such loving condescension and a love so condescending" (LM 9,2).

74. 1Cel 115.
75. 2Cel 11.
76. 2Cel 10.
77. Ibid.
78. LM 8,1.
79. Fior, Consideration III.
80. Ibid.
81. LM 13,3.
82. Consideration III.
83. Ibid.
84. LM 14,4. For this topic see O. Schmucki, *Das Leiden Christi im Leben des hl. Franziskus von Assisi* (Rome, 1960).
85. S. Clasen, "Das Heiligkeitsideal im Wandeln der Zeiten," in *Wissenschaft und Weisheit* 33 (1970), pp. 133–64, 142.
86. For a theory of the feminine and the masculine, see L. Boff, *El Rostro Materno de Dios*, 2nd edition (Madrid, 1980).
87. C. Esser, "Libertad para el amor," in *Temas espirituales* (Oñate, Spain, 1980), pp. 121–38; E. Rohr, *Der Herr und Franziskus* (Werl/West, 1966), pp. 214–21.
88. Adm 16; 1R 22; 2R 10.
89. See the following for this subject: J. M. Erikson, *Saint Francis and His Four Ladies* (New York, 1970); A. Zarri, "Francesco e Chiara: una proposta," in *Francesco e Altro* (Rome, 1976), pp. 145–64; E. Romagnolo, "La donna nella vita e nel pensiero di Francesco d'Assisi," in *Francesco d'Assisi nel 750° anno della morte (1226–1976)* (Jerusalem, 1976); L.-A. Djari, "Un saint pour temps de crise," in *Evangile aujourd'hui* 69 (1971), pp. 51–57; C. A. Lainati, "Clara, la mujer de la esperanza," in *Selecciones de franciscanismo* 2 (1973), pp. 127–34.
90. D. Eclid, *Clara de Asís: La hermana ideal de San Francisco* (Madrid, 1981), pp. 132–36.
91. For basic biographical data, see Omer Englebert, *Vida de san Francisco de Asís* (Santiago, 1974), pp. 186–205 [*Saint Francis of Assisi*, 2nd English ed. (Chicago, 1965)].
92. I. Omaechevarria, *Escritos de Santa Clara y documentos contemporáneos* (Madrid, 1970).
93. Ibid.
94. Ibid.
95. Cf. W. Nigg, *O Homen de Assis* (Petropolis, 1975), pp. 32–33; Mario von Galli, *Gelebte Zukunft: Franz von Assisi* (Lucerne and Frankfurt, 1970), p. 181.
96. See the beautiful commentary by W. Nigg, *O Homem de Assis*, p. 33.
97. Process of Canonization III, 29, in I. Omaechevarria, *Escritos de Santa Clara y documentos contemporáneos* (Madrid, 1970).
98. Legend of St. Clare 7–9: "She surrendered her heart to St. Francis and Francis in turn consecrated her to God" (P. Robinson, *The Life of St. Clare* [London, 1915], p. 36).
99. Rule of Saint Clare I, 3; Testament of Saint Clare, 49; MP 108.
100. Legend of Saint Clare 14.
101. Rule of Saint Clare VI, 3–5.
102. LM 12,2; Fior 16.
103. Cf. C. A. Lainati, "Clara aconseja a Francisco," in *Selecciones de franciscanismo* 2 (1973), pp. 171–77.
104. Fior 15.
105. LP 109.
106. See C. R. Urner, *The Search for Brother Jacoba: A Study on Jacoba dei Sette-*

soli, Friend of Francis of Assisi and His Movement (Manila, xerox copy, 1980), pp. 146–50; H. M. Castiglione, *Frate Jacoba* (Rome, 1933); E. Ameni, *Giacomina Settesoli* (Florence, 1933).

107. 1R 13.

108. 2Cel 112; cf. Fior 15, where the brothers scold him for his excessive rigor.

109. Here it is good to reflect on the gentle love that Francis felt for the Virgin Mary. See the important study by C. Esser, "La devoción a Maria Santísima en San Francisco de Asís," in *Temas espirituales*, pp. 281–309; C. Koser, *O Pensamento Franciscano* (Petropolis, 1960), pp. 47–55.

110. 2Cel 131.

111. Ibid., 137.

112. LP 5; MP 28; 2Cel 176.

113. Darmstadt Manuscript (XIV Century) cited by O. Englebert, *Life of Saint Francis of Assisi*, p. 145.

114. 2R 6; 1R 9.

115. Rule for Hermits 1 and 10.

116. LM 8,5.

117. 2Cel 177.

118. 1Cel 3.

119. Ibid.

120. Ibid.

121. LM 8,1.

122. 1Cel 81.

123. 2Cel 134; 165. Among the many titles on this material, see: M. de Marzi, *San Francesco d'Assisi e l'ecologia* (Rome, mimeograph, 1981), with a valuable bibliography; E. A. Armstrong, *Saint Francis: Nature Mystic: The Derivation and Significance of the Nature Stories in the Franciscan Legend* (Berkeley, Los Angeles and London, 1976); J. Lang, "Erschaut und Begriffen: Die sakramentale Genialität das hl. Franziskus von Assisi," in *Wissenschaft und Weisheit*, 40 (1977), 1–10; Francis Cuthbert, *The Romanticism of St. Francis* (London, 1915); I. Wilges, "São Francisco de Assis e a ecologia," in *O Franciscanismo no Mundo de Hoje* (Petropolis, 1981), pp. 84–96.

124. MP 113.

125. 2Cel 165.

126. Ibid. 212.

127. Ibid. 165.

128. Ibid.

129. Armstrong showed that the influences upon Francis may stem from the love of nature and the "gay science" of Provence, may stem from the Irish tradition, from the monks and pilgrims who had a very positive relationship with nature (*Saint Francis: Nature Mystic*, pp. 18–43).

130. 2Cel 165; LM 8,6.

131. LM 5,9.

132. 2Cel 171.

133. LM 8,9.

134. Eloi Leclerc, *The Canticle of the Creatures* (Chicago, 1977), pp. 240–48.

135. Cf. some of the more significant titles dealing with the understanding of humanity and of the world of Saint Francis: S. Verhey, *Der Mensch unter der Herrschaft Gottes: Versuch einer Theologie des Menschen nach dem hl. Franziskus von Assisi* (Düsseldorf, 1969); R. Koper, *Das Weltverständnis des hl. Franziskus von Assisi* (Werl/West, 1959); M. Auerbach, "Über das Persönliche in der Wirkung des hl. Franziskus von Assisi," in *Gesammelte Aufsätze zur romanischen Philologie* (Berna, 1967).

136. See L. Boff, "A pobreza no mistério do homen e de Cristo," in *Grande Sinal* 27 (1973), pp. 163–83; H. Schaluck, *Armut und Heil* (Paderborn, 1971).

137. The best study on conversion is still that of F. Beer, *Le conversion de Saint François selon Thomas de Celano* (Paris, 1963).

138. LM 8,1.

139. The bibliography is immense; we point out some of the more important titles: L. Bracaloni, *Il Cantico di Frate Sole* (Milan, 1927); E. W. Platzeck, *Das Sonnelied des heiligen Franziskus von Assisi* (Munich, 1957); G. Getto, *San Francesco d'Assisi e il Cantico di Frate Sole* (Turin, 1956); G. Sabatelli, "Studi recenti sul Cantico di Frate Sole," in *Archivum Franciscanum Historicum* 51 (1958), pp. 3–24; M. de Marzi, *San Francesco d'Assisi e l'ecologia* (Rome, 1981), pp. 104–19; the most original contribution, however, is that of Eloi Leclerc, *The Canticle of the Creatures*.

140. L. Scheffcyck, "Der Sonnengesang des hl. Franziskus von Assisi und der Hymne an die Materie des Teilhard de Chardin," in *Geist und Leben* 35 (1962), pp. 219–33.

141. LP 43; MP 100.

142. LM 14,1–2.

143. 2Cel 213.

144. Eloi Leclerc, *The Canticle of the Creatures*, p. 16.

145. Ibid., esp. 25–48; each chapter is introduced by a hermeneutical reflection.

146. Paul Sabatier, Daniel Rops, and others try to see Clare as the inspiration for the Canticle of Brother Sun, because she was the one who took care of Francis during his illness at San Damiano, where Francis wrote the hymn. Paul Sabatier came to imagine an absent verse, dedicate to Clare: *"Soyez loué, Seigneur, pour souer Claire; nous l'avez faite silencieuse, active et subtile; et par elle votre lumière brille dans nos coeurs."* For this, see Armindo Augusto, "A enfermidade do poeta cego," in *Louvor de Santa Clara* (Braga, 1954), pp. 270–87, here p. 286.

147. Eloi Leclerc, *The Canticle*, pp. 243–50: "The Poetry of Salvation."

Chapter 2—Preferential Option for the Poor

1. The social pyramid of Brazil presents the following shameful picture: 1% very rich; 4% rich; 15% with the necessities of life (middle class); 30% semi-poor (working class) and 50% poor (below working class).

2. *A Evangelização no Presente e no Futuro de América Latina* (Petropolis, 1979), nos. 88 and 89; cf. summary in nos. 1207–8. John Kenneth Galbraith, *A Natureza da Pobreza das Massas* (Rio de Janeiro, 1979), p. 27 [*The Nature of Mass Poverty* (Cambridge, Mass., 1979], recognizing that "poverty is the greatest and most destructive tormentor of man. It is at the core of many other sufferings—from hunger and disease to civil conflict and war itself. . . . However, for the poverty that brings about such conflict, we have no explanation. Or, more precisely, we have a plethora of explanations, each one superficially persuasive, offered as true, and each one notable because it does not explain it absolutely."

3. This does not mean simply to take the wealth from the rich and distribute it among the poor. It would not be enough for everyone. This type of argument is used with bad intentions by the rich and their allies, to make impossible, because of its ridiculousness, any reform. The question is not to redistribute the wealth of the rich, but rather to produce goods by all and for all, making less and more tolerable the distance between one another. All must work for the reproduction of social life. The costs and benefits must be distributed as equitably as possible among all.

4. For centuries, a naturistic and substantialistic conception of society predominated, as something given and already determined by the creative act of God. And so it was said: it is the will of nature and, in the end, the will of God that there be rich and poor; the rich are saved through generosity and the poor through patience. The lack of vision as to the causal link between poverty and wealth led, inevitably, to resignation and compromise, and from there to social immobility, favoring the rich and perpetuating the pains and injustices of the poor. With the advent of historical consciousness, it is understood that society is a project and, as such, something historically constructed through the centuries, mutable, trusted to the responsibility of humanity, authors of society and of history.

5. Puebla, no. 30; John Paul II, *Discurso Inaugural a los Obispos en Puebla*, III,3;

see "Letter to the Christians that live and celebrate their faith in the popular Christian communities of the countries and poor regions of the world," in *Puebla* 7 (1980), pp. 430–33, esp. 430: "And together we saw that the poverty existent in Latin America and in the rest of the world is not the result of destiny, but of a great injustice that shouts to heaven, like the blood of Abel murdered by Cain (Gen 4:10). We also saw that the principal cause of this injustice must be sought in the capitalist system that, like a new Tower of Babel (Gen 11:1–8) rises over the world and controls the life of the peoples, favoring some who each day grow richer at the side of the growing poverty of others. Because of this, the impoverished peoples of our countries live in a true captivity within their own land." The letter is the conclusion of the International Ecumenical Congress of Theology, held in São Paulo in February–March 1981.

6. The phrase of President John F. Kennedy, citing Attlee, is well-known: "If a free society cannot help the many who are poor, it cannot save the few who are rich": cf. D. N. Lott, *The Inaugural Addresses of the American Presidents from Washington to Kennedy* (New York, 1961), p. 270.

7. Cf. N. Rodrigues, *Os Africanos no Brasil* (Sao Paulo, 1932); M. Goulart, *A Escravidão Africana no Brasil* (Sao Paulo, 1975); L. Luna, *O Negro na Luta Contra a Escradidão* (Rio De Janeiro, 1976).

8. Cf. J. N. Rodrigues, *Conciliação e Reforma no Brasil* (Rio de Janeiro, 1965), pp. 23–111.

9. M. Mollat, *Les pauvres au moyen-age* (Paris, 1978), p. 14.

10. F. Houtart, "Le religion dans la formation sociale de la Palestine du premier siècle et l'acteur socio-religieux Jésus," in *Religion et modes de production précapitalistes* (Brussels, 1980), pp. 218–53, here 245: "According to modern studies, 'Jesus of Nazareth is a prophet coming from the circles of the scribes and the Pharisees. Although he criticizes them theoretically, he maintains the fundamental elements of ideological production, to such an extent that, often, he is confused with them. . . . His social class is that of the small artisan bourgeoisie. But Jesus does not primarily direct his practice to this social category. On the contrary, his social base is made up of the masses at the margin of the process of production and by the mass of illiterate farmers and the most exploited, all who receive the name of *am ha-ares.' "

11. Of the "notables" of Jerusalem (Gal 2:2), James, Cephas, and John, to whom Paul presented his gospel directed to the Gentiles, received the approbation with the following recommendation: "That we become one with the poor, and I took that to heart" (Gal 2:10; cf. Acts 11:29–30).

12. See the detailed investigation by Clodovis Boff on the Church and the poor through the centuries that will be published shortly. One of the chapters was published in *Puebla* 7 (1980), pp. 385–402: "A Opção Preferencial pelos Pobres durante mil anos de história da Igreja."

13. E. Troeltsch, *The Social Teaching of the Christian Churches*, vol. 1 (London and New York, 1950), p. 51. For this subject see the collective work of J. Dupont, A. George, B. Rigaux, and others, *La pobreza evangélica hoy* (Bogota, 1971). Clement of Alexandria posed, in his time, the question correctly: *Quis dives salvetur?*—translated "Can the rich man be saved?"—responding in terms of moral change and not social change: The rich are saved in the measure that they use wealth to do more charity and so diminish poverty.

14. Vozes edition (Petropolis, 1976), V, 13–17; the same thing is testified to by the great critic of Christianism, the philosopher Celsus, who finds motives for scorning the Christians because they are people of low rent, artisans, porters, servants, maids, cobblers, etc. See J. de Santa Ana, *A Igreja e o Desafio dos Pobres* (Petropolis, 1980), pp. 90–91.

15. The best work on this subject seems to be that of P. Richard, *Mort des chrètientés et naissance de l'Eglise* (Paris, 1978).

16. This statement must be understood in its general and dominant sense, be-

cause, specifically, there was also a consciousness that the poor can help themselves as can be seen in this homily of Saint Basil: "Drink the water of your cistern (Prov 5:15), that is, consider your means, do not ask from the distant spring but see in your own waters the sustenance of your life. Have jars of bronze, clothing, a horse, some furniture. Sell them, accept anything save losing your freedom. You may say that it is hard to carry them to auction. . . . Do not knock at other doors. The neighbor's well is always narrow (Prov 23:27). It is better to meet your needs with your work than to get up suddenly, thanks to the help of another, only to lose all of your goods. If you have money, why not use your resources to relieve your misery? And if you have nothing, why cure an evil, causing another? Do not deliver yourself to the usurer who will harm you, nor let yourself be chased and caught like a prisoner": *Homily II on Psalm 15; PG* 29, 263ff.

17. The basic reference work is the book by M. Mollat, *Les pauvres au moyen-age* and its creative summary in Clodovis Boff, "A Opção Preferencial pelos Pobres."

18. He was the Pope with the most power in the Church, with a pessimistic vision of human existence (cf. *De miseria humanae conditionis*), but with acute sensitivity for the poor. He founded the Hospital of the Holy Spirit and started fraternities dedicated to service to the poor. He donated to the poor the gifts offered at the Basilica of Saint Peter and there were times when he alone fed close to 8,000 indigents daily; see L. Lallemand, *Histoire de la charité*, III (Paris, 1906), p. 306; M. Mollat, "Hospitalité et assistance au début du XIIIème siècle," in D. Flood (ed.), *Poverty in the Middle Ages* (Werl/West, 1975), pp. 37–51, here p. 39.

19. See the important study of Yves Congar, "Una realidad tradicional: la Iglesia, recurso de los débiles y de los pobres," in *Eglise et pauvreté* (Paris, 1965), pp. 258–66). Saint Bernard reminds Pope Innocent II: "If you observe your apostolic duty and ancient custom, you cannot reject the cause of the poor, nor side with the powerful."

20. *Eorum qui pauperes opprimunt, donaria sacerdotibus refutanda:* see the other study by Congar, "Los bienes temporales de la Iglesia según la tradición teológica y canónica," in *Eglise et pauvreté*, pp. 233–58.

21. Cf. M. Mollat, *Hospitalité et assistance*, pp. 37–51.

22. G. Couvreur, *Les pauvres ont-ils des droits?: Recherches sur le vol en cas d'extreme nècessité despuis la Concordia de Gratien (1140) jusqu'à a Guillaume d'Auxerre (1231)* (Rome and Paris, 1961), p. 257.

23. *Iure naturae omnia sunt communia, i.e., tempore necessitatis sunt communicanda.*

24. M. Mollat, *Les pauvres*, pp. 129–42; see also G. Dubuy, "Les pauvres des campagnes dans l'Occident médièval," in *Revue d'Histoire de l'Eglise de France* 52 (1966), pp. 25–32. During the time of the quarrels between mendicants and seculars in Paris the distinction between the *Christus largiens* (who gives) and the *Christus accipiens* (who receives) was in vogue.

25. The classic work, in terms of an idealist interpretation, is that of G. Grundmann, *Religiöse Bewegungen im Mittelalter* (Hildesheim, 1961); see the criticism by D. Flood, "The Grundmann Approach to Early Franciscan Poverty," in *Franziskanische Studien* 59 (1977), pp. 311–19; J. L. Nelson presents an alternative vision in "Society, Theodicy and the Origins of Heresy: Towards a Reassessment of the Medieval Evidence," in *Schism, Heresy and Religious Protest*, ed. D. Baker (Cambridge, 1972), pp. 65–77; also L. K. Little, "Evangelical Poverty, the New Money Economy and Violence," in *Poverty in the Middle Ages*, pp. 11–26; an older work, but methodologically suggestive is that of J. B. Pierron, *Die katholischen Armen: Ein Beitrag zur Entstehungsgeschichte der Bettlerorden mit Berücksichtigung der Humiliaten und der Wiedervereinigten Lombarden* (Frieburg, 1911).

26. *Das Kapital*, pt. 3, VIII, XIII; pt. 7, XXIV; see also L. Hubermann, *História da riqueza do homem* (Rio de Janeiro, 1981), all of chapter XVI, pp. 187–206.

27. For this part see M. D. Chenu, *La dottrina della Chiesa: Origine e sviluppo (1891–1971)* (Brescia, 1977), pp. 48–53.

28. C. Boff, "A Opção Preferencial pelos Pobres," pp. 400–401.

29. For a development of this subject see L. Boff, *O Caminhar da Igreja com os Oprimidos* (Rio de Janeiro, 1980).

30. Nos. 1134–65; cf. the excellent commentaries by Gustavo Gutiérrez, *A Força Histórica dos Pobres* (Petropolis, 1981), pp. 194–231; J. Simoes Jorge, *Puebla, Libertação do Homem Pobre* (Sao Paulo, 1981).

31. This perspective was stressed by the Pope in his speeches in the Philippines: cf. *L'Osservatore Romano*, August 3, 1981, p. 5.

32. D. Aloisio Lorscheider, Cardinal of Fortaleza, Brazil says pointedly: "Many have not come to understand that the Church changed its social position. The Church reads social reality, beginning from another angle. It moved from the social level of the elites to the social position of the people. The people . . . are the poor and simple and from this position it made the preferential option for the poor. The Church sees the reality and desires to renew the world from the place of the poor" (*Jornal do Brasil*, November 2, 1981).

33. Enrique Dussel, *De Medellín a Puebla: Una década de sangre y esperanza* (Mexico City, 1979).

34. Cf. my exposition in *O Caminhar da Igreja com os Oprimidos*, pp. 129–35.

35. No. 1135, footnote 331.

36. Cf. the important work of P. Gauthier, *O Concilio e a Igreja dos Pobres* (Petropolis, 1967), pp. 111–60.

37. Cf. L. Boff, *Teologia do Cautiveiro e da Libertaço* (Petropolis, 1979), pp. 221–39.

38. Puebla, no. 1142: "whatever the moral or personal situation in which they find themselves . . ."; J. Dupont, "Los pobres y la pobreza en los Evangelios y en los Hechos," in *La Pobreza evangelica Hoy*, p. 37.

39. Gustavo Gutiérrez also calls it the path of spiritual childhood in his *Teologia da Libertação* (Petropolis, 1975), pp. 234–49 [*A Theology of Liberation* (Maryknoll, 1973)].

40. Joachim Jeremias, "Quiénes son los pobres para Jesús," in *Teología del Nuevo Testamento* (Salamanca, 1974), pp. 134–38 [*New Testament Theology* (New York)].

41. "Die religiöse Bewegungen des Hochmittelalters und Franz von Assisi," in *Festgabe F. J. Lortz*, II (Baden-Baden, 1958), pp. 287–315, here p. 292.

42. H. Grundmann, *Religiöse Bewegungen*, pp. 59–61.

43. C. Esser, "Die religiöse Bewegungen," p. 299.

44. H. Grundmann, *Religiöse Bewegungen*, pp. 164–65.

45. I. Silveira, "S. Francisco e a burguesia," in *Nosso Irmão Francisco de Assis* (Petropolis, 1975), pp. 35–36; C. Esser, *La Orden Franciscana: Orígenes e Ideales* (Aranzazu, 1976), pp. 62–71 [*Origins of the Franciscan Order* (Chicago, 1970)].

46. M. Vovk, "Die franziskanische 'Fraternitas' als Erfüllung eines Anliegens der Hochmittelalterlichen Zeit," in *Wissenschaft und Weisheit* 39 (1976), pp. 2–25, esp. 21.

47. TC 2.

48. Cf. A. Fortini, *Nova Vita di San Francesco*, II (Assisi, 1959), pp. 115–16; I, pp. 113–29 [*Francis of Assisi* (New York, 1980)].

49. TC 2.

50. LM 1,1.

51. 1Cel 3.

52. Lm 1,2; 1Cel 17; 2Cel 5; 8.

53. 1Cel 17.

54. TC 9.

55. 1Cel 14; cf. 9.

56. LM 1,2.

57. 1Cel 13–15.

58. 1Cel 17.

59. Lm 1,6; 2Cel 9.

60. 1Cel 21.
61. It could have been October 12, 1208 (Feast of St. Luke), or February 24, 1209 (Feast of St. Matthias), when the gospel of the sending out of the apostles by Jesus was read.
62. 1Cel 22.
63. 1Cel 76; cf. 51, 55, 119, 135.
64. Test 1–3; cf. H. Tilemann, *Studien zur Individualität des Franziskus von Assisi* (Leipzig-Berlin, 1974), pp. 131–40.
65. For the different meanings of world in Saint Francis see the work of R. Koper, *Das Weltverständnis des hl. Franziskus von Assisi* (Werl/West, 1959).
66. MP 58.
67. Cf. Let0 3; LetSup 1; LetF 1.
68. See Thomas of Spoleto, in *St. Francis of Assisi: Omnibus of Sources*, p. 1601; 1Cel 83; Fior 10.
69. 2R 1,1; see some of the more significant titles: M. D. Lambert, *Franciscan Poverty: The Doctrine of the Absolute Poverty of Christ and the Apostles in the Franciscan Order 1210–1323* (London, 1961); B. O'Mahony, "Franciscan Poverty Yesterday and Today," in *Laurentianum* 10 (1969), pp. 37–64; E. Esser, "Mysterium paupertatis," in *Temas espirituales*, pp. 73–96; E. Esser, "Die Armutsauffassung des hl. Franziskus," in D. Flood (ed.), *Poverty in the Middle Ages*, pp. 60–70.
70. Saint Bonaventure, *De perfectione evangelica*, Quaest. II ad 2 (*Opera Omnia V*, 148).
71. 2R 2,16; 1R 2,14.
72. 2R 6; 1R 8.
73. Testament; cf. 2Cel 59.
74. 2Cel 20; LM 8.
75. 2R 2; 2Cel 80.
76. 2R 3; only the breviary is mentioned. The rest are found in 1R 3,7 and LetMin.
77. 2Cel 194.
78. 1R 17.
79. Adm 4.
80. 1R 2.
81. Adm 9.
82. Adm 14.
83. SalVir.
84. Adm 19.
85. 1R 17,17–18; "We must refer every good to the most high supreme God, acknowledge that all good belongs to him; and we must thank him for it all, because all good comes from him. May the most supreme and high and only true God receive and have all."
86. 1R 23.
87. See L. Iriarte, "Appropriatio et Expropriatio in doctrina S. Francisci," in *Laurentianum* 11 (1970), pp. 3–35, giving all references.
88. Ibid.
89. Cited by Cajetan Esser, *La Orden Franciscana: Orígenes e ideales*, p. 187.
90. See the testimony of the famous chronicler and cardinal Jacques de Vitry, in *St. Francis of Assisi: Omnibus of Sources*, p. 1609.
91. 2Cel 148.
92. For this entire subject see Cajetan Esser, *La Orden Franciscana*, pp. 335–51.
93. Testament of Siena.
94. M. Bernards, "Nudus nudum sequi," in *Wissenschaft und Weisheit* 14 (1951), pp. 148ff.
95. 1R 9; 2R 6.
96. 2Cel 56.
97. The entire second part of chaps. 27–38; also 2Cel 80–93.
98. 2Cel 91.

99. 1R 2; 2Cel 56, passim.
100. Ibid. 37.
101. TC 34.
102. *Sein und Zeit*, pt. I, chap. 6, pp. 41–42; pt. II, chap. 3, p. 64.
103. 2R 6; 1R 9.
104. Ibid., 9; 2R 3. The same phrase is used by the famous theologian of the time, Peter of Cantor, *Unum ex quattuor 69: nec eger solvens ieiunium peccat, necessitas enim non habet legem.* The manuscript was published by G. Couvreur, *Les pauvres ont-ils des droits?* (Rome, 1961), p. 157; footnote 17.
105. 2R 6; 1R 10.
106. 1Cel 39.
107. *Der unvergleichliche Heilige* (Dusseldorf, 1952).
108. Cf. 2Cel 85.
109. LM 12,2; Fior 16.
110. Cajetan Esser offers a good vision of community in *La Orden Franciscana*, pp. 185–267.
111. A. Rotzetter, *Die Funktion der franziskanischen Bewegung in der Kirche* (Tau-Verlag, Switzerland, 1977), pp. 282–89.
112. D. Flood, "Domestication of the Franciscan Movement," in *Franziscanischen Studien* 60 (1978), pp. 311–27.
113. See my short study, L. Boff, *Pueblas Herausforderung an die Franziskaner* (Bonn, 1980).
114. LP 114.
115. Cf. MP 68; LM 11,3; TC 6,17, etc.

Chapter 3—Liberation through Goodness

1. For this subject see the classic work of Gustavo Gutierrez, *Teologia da Libertação* (Petropolis, 1975); see also the writings of L. Boff, *Teologia da Libertação e do Cativeiro* (Petropolis, 1979), and *O Caminhar da Igreja com os Oprimidos* (Rio de Janeiro, 1980).
2. More detailed in Enrique Dussel, *Filosofía de la Liberación* (Mexico City, 1977).
3. Cf. Gustavo Gutiérrez, "Teologia a partir do reverso da história," in *A Força Histórica dos Pobres* (Petropolis, 1981), pp. 245–313.
4. The best work on this subject is that of Clodovis Boff, *Teologia e Prática: A teologia do político e suas mediaçoês* (Petropolis, 1981).
5. Pablo Neruda, *Confieso que he vivido* (Barcelona, 1981), pp. 238–39 [*Memoirs* (New York, 1976)].
6. See the detailed study by R. Muñoz, *Evangelio y liberación en América Latina* (Bogota, 1980).
7. H. Roggen, "Hizo Francisco una opción de clase?" in *Selecciones de Teología* 3 (1974), pp. 287–95, here p. 288.
8. See F. Ferrarotti, *La società come problema e come progetto* (Milan, 1979), esp. pp. 323–30.
9. Due to a lack of epistemological consciousness, many analyses, although meticulous from the historical point of view, are insufficient because they do not say all they could tell; this happens with H. Roggen, "Die Lebensform des hl. Franziskus von Assisi in ihrem Verhältnis zur feudalen und bürgerlichen Gesellschaft Italiens," in *Franziskanische Studien* 46 (1964), pp. 1–57, 287–321; S. Clasen, "Franziskus von Assisi und die soziale Frage," in *Wissenschaft und Weisheit* 15 (1952), pp. 109–21; good treatments include I. Silveira, "S. Francisco e a burguesia," in *Nosso Irmão Francisco de Assis* (Petropolis, 1975), pp. 11–63; H. J. Stiker, Un createur en son temps: François d'Assise," in *Christus* 80 (1973), pp. 416–30; and P. Anasagasti, *Liberación en San Francisco de Asís* (Aranzazu, 1976), among others.
10. For this entire complex of questions see the bibliographically rich study of

M. Vovk, "Die franziskanische 'Fraternitas' als Erfüllung eines Angliens der Hochmittelalterlichen Zeit," in *Wissenschaft und Weisheit* 39 (1976), pp. 2–25, esp. 3–7.

11. Cf. H. Pirenne, *Storia economica e sociale del medioevo* (Milan, 1967), II, pp. 53–74; G. A. J. Hodgett, *História Social e Económica da Idade Media* (Rio de Janeiro, 1975), pp. 106–26, 192–213.

12. The importance of the "new" category was put in relief by the work of D.-M. Chenu, *La théologie au douzième siècle* (Paris, 1957), pp. 323–65.

13. H. Grundmann, *Religiöse Bewegungen im Mittelalter* (Hildesheim, 1961), p. 14.

14. J. Lortz, *Geschichte der Kirche in ideengeschichtlicher Betrachtung*, I (Munster, 1965), pp. 328–36.

15. Cf. K. L. Little, "Evangelical Poverty, the New Money Economy and Violence," in D. Flood (ed.), *Poverty in the Middle Ages* (Werl/West, 1975), pp. 11–26.

16. Grundmann, *Religiöse Bewegungen*, pp. 508ff.

17. LP 114; MP 119: *Et dixit mihi Dominus, quod volebat quod ego essem novellus pazzus in mundo.*

18. TC 19; 1Cel 43: he remains indifferent when the Emperor Otto passes by his hut in Rivo Torto, "in spite of the noise and pomp"; he only sends a brother to remind him of the fleeting nature of temporal power.

19. A. Fortini, *Nova Vita di San Francesco* (Assisi, 1959), pp. 357–60.

20. MP 12.

21. Dealing with the determinations 16 and 18 of the *Propositum*.

22. See the detailed study of A. Rotzetter, "Kreuzzugskritik und Ablehnung der Feudalordnung in der Gefolgschaft des Franziskus von Assisi," in *Wissenschaft und Weisheit* 35 (1972), pp. 121–37.

23. A. Rotzetter, "Der utopische Entwurf der franziskanischen Gemeinschaft," in *Wissenschaft und Weisheit* 37 (1974), pp. 159–69; D. Cervera, "Ensayo sobre la actualidad de Francisco de Aís," in *Verdad y Vida* 34 (1976), pp. 388–410.

24. 1R 5; 22.

25. Adm 4; LetF.

26. MP 72.

27. 1R 5. There are three levels of obedience in the thought of Saint Francis. The first refers to interpersonal relationships in terms of desire, will, need of the other that each one must respond to with sensitivity and attention, being available and at the service of the other (1R 5 and 16). On the second level, obedience refers to the relationship between the superiors and their charges but with a typically Franciscan version: the superior must be obedient to his subordinates; he is the servant and the others are lords (c. 10). Finally, the conventional meaning: obedience of the subordinate to his superior who, for Francis, is only the minister or guardian.

28. 1R 5.

29. Ibid., 14.

30. Ibid., 16.

31. The celebrated book of the great Brasilian educator Paulo Freire, of the same title: *Pedagogia do Oprimido* (Rio de Janeiro, 1975) [*Pedagogy of the Oppressed* (New York, 1971)].

32. Fior 37; LM 5,7.

33. L. Iriarte, *Vocación Franciscana* (Valencia, 1975), p. 171.

34. TC 35. For this topic see the in-depth study by L. Thier, "Der Friede erwächst aus der Armut," in *Wissenschaft und Weisheit* 39 (1976), pp. 108–22; L. Robinot, "Saint François chante le pardon des offenses," in *Evangile aujourd'hui* 77 (1973), pp. 47–55.

35. 1Cel 23.

36. TC 39.

37. 1R 7.

38. TC 58.

39. 2Cel 37.

40. Thomas of Spoleto, in *St. Francis of Assisi: Omnibus of Sources*, p. 1601.

41. 2Cel 108.
42. Fior 11.
43. The entire story is found in detail in MP 101.
44. Ibid.
45. 1Cel 57; LM 9,7-9; LP 37; Fior 24. The best study of the topic continues to be that of I. Lemmens, "De sancto Francisco Christum praedicante coram Sultano Aegypti," in *Archivum Franciscanum Historicum* 19 (1926), pp. 559-78.
46. 2Cel 30.
47. Cf. Cajetan Esser, "Franziskus von Assisi und die Katherer seiner Zeit," in *Archivum Franciscanum Historicum* 51 (1958), pp. 225-64.
48. LP 90; MP 66.
49. Fior 21.
50. This perspective was clearly perceived by A. Bergamaschi, "Saint François, Gubbio, le loup et la lutte des classes," in *Etudes Franciscaines* 15 (1965), pp. 84-92 which inspired this exegesis.
51. Eloi Leclerc, *Destierro y Ternura* (Madrid, 1967), p. 17 [*Exile and Tenderness* (Chicago, 1965)].
52. LM prologue 1.
53. Ibid.
54. LM 3,2.
55. LM 3,7.
56. 1Cel 23.
57. 1Cel 120.
58. A. Rotzetter, "Die weltzugewandte Spiritualität des Franz von Assisi—eine Provokation für heute," in *Diakonia* 7 (1976), pp. 30-37.
59. LP 114.
60. Cf. L. Izzo, *La semplicità evangelica nella spiritualità di S. Francesco d'Assisi* (Rome, 1971), pp. 185-207.
61. SC 63.
62. 1R 22; Letter to Brother Leo.
63. 2R 2,7.
64. All of the passages were collected and analyzed by A. Rotzetter, "Der franziskanische Mensch zwischen Autorität und Freiheit," in *Franziskanische Studien* 59 (1977), pp. 97-124, esp. 120-21.
65. 2Cel 193; cf. G. Pagliara, *Incontro a Dio Amore: Itinerario di spiritualità francescana* (Assisi, 1979), pp. 301-25.
66. 1R 10.
67. 2R 2.
68. LP 97.
69. Ibid.; cf. 96.
70. LP 95.
71. Letter to a Minister.
72. Cf. L. Lavelle, *Spiritualità francescana* (Milan, 1967), pp. 30-35.
73. "True and Perfect Joy," in *St. Francis of Assisi: Omnibus of Sources*, p. 174.
74. SalVir.

Chapter 4—Creation of a Popular and Poor Church

1. P. Richard, *Mort des chretientes e naissance de l'Eglise* (Paris, 1978).
2. Y. Congar, *L'ecclesiologie du haut moyen-age* (Paris, 1968), p. 97; A. Faivre, *Naissance d'une hierarchie* (Paris, 1977), pp. 411-23.
3. The dynamic of this process was competently studied from the point of view of the sociology of religion by P. Bourdie, *A Economia das Trocas Simbolicas* (San Paulo, 1947), pp. 27-78, esp. pp. 39ff., and O. Maduro, *Religiao e Luta de Classes* (Petropolis, 1981), pp. 125-36.

4. In popular language: He is a layman in the matter.

5. See the texts alluded to in Y. Congar, *L'ecclesiologie*, p. 389; id., "Le monotheisme politique et le Dieu Trinite," in *Nouvelle Revue Theologique* 103 (1981), pp. 3–17.

6. Ibid., pp. 81–85, 190–195, 267–271.

7. C. 7, c. XII, q. 1.

8. For a theological understanding of the founding desire of Jesus and the place of the ministers within the Church, see L. Boff, *Eclesiogenese* (Petropolis, 1977), pp. 47–73, with the cited bibliography.

9. Especially *Lumen Gentium;* cf. the best collection of studies on the Church of Vatican II, of the same title, edited by G. Barauna (Petropolis, 1965); B. Kloppenburg, *A Eclesiologia do Vaticano II* (Petropolis, 1972).

10. A. Acerbi, *Due ecclesiologie: Ecclesiologie giuridica ed ecclesiologia di communione nella Lumen Gentium* (Bologne, 1975).

11. A. Ribeiro Guimaraes, *Comunidades de Base no Brasil* (Petropolis, 1978).

12. Cf. H. Salem, *Igreja dos Oprimidos* (Rio de Janeiro, 1981); L. Boff, *O Caminhar da Igreja com os Oprimidos* (Rio de Janeiro, 1980).

13. Cl. Boff, *Comunidade Crista-Comunidade Política* (Petropolis, 1978).

14. L. Boff, *Igreja: Carisma e Poder* (Petropolis, 1981).

15. See the entire issue of *Concilium* 157 (1980), dedicated to the participation of the local Church in the choosing of bishops.

16. G. Hasenhuttl, *Chrisma Ordnungsprinzip der Kirche* (Freiburg-Vienna, 1969).

17. J. de Santa Ana, *A Igreja e o Desafio dos Pobres* (Petropolis, 1980), pp. 133–49; J. Moltmann, *La Iglesia, fuerza del Espiritu* (Salamanca, 1978), pp. 157–61 [*The Church in the Power of the Spirit* (New York, 1977)].

18. On the topic there exists an ample bibliography, as can be seen in *Collectanea Franciscana* XIII (1964–1973), pp. 841–44; see especially C. Esser "Sancta Mater Ecclesia Romana: La piedad eclesial de s. Francisco," in *Temas espirituales* (Oñate, 1980), pp. 139–88; O. Schmucki, "Franziskus von Assisi erfahrt Kirche in seiner Bruderschaft," in *Franziskanische Studien* 58 (1976) pp. 1–26; A. Rotzetter, *Die Funktion der franziskanischen Bewegung in der Kirche* (Schwyz/Achweiz, 1977); E. Benz, *Ecclesia spiritualis: Kirchenidee und Geschichtstheologie der franziskanischen Reformation* (Stuttgart, 1934).

19. His *Vie de Saint François* (Paris, 1893) is, despite all the criticisms, one of the most brilliant biographies of the Poverello.

20. C. Esser, "Sancta Mater Ecclesia Romana"; for this whole question see the studies of K. Selge, "Franz von Assisi und die romische Kurie," in *Zeitschrift für Theologie und Kirche* 67 (1970), pp. 129–61; by the same author, "Franz von Assisi und Hugolino von Ostia," in *San Francesco nella ricerca historica degli ultimi ottanta anni* (Convegni del Centro di studi sulla spiritualità medievale, October 13–16, 1968; Todi, 1971), pp. 157–222.

21. M. Maccarrone, "San Francesco e la Chiesa di Inocenzo III," in *Aproccio storico-critico alle Fonti Francescane* (Rome, 1979), pp. 31–43.

22. Cf. I. Silveira, "São Francisco e a burguesia," in *Nosso Irmao Francisco de Assis* (Petropolis, 1957), pp. 11–47, esp. pp. 17–20.

23. Cf. H. Grundmann, *Religiöse Bewegungen in Mittelalter* (Hildesheim, 1961), pp. 10–11, 50–69.

24. LP 8.

25. MP 26.

26. 1R 6.

27. Ibid., 7.

28. J. Ratzinger, "Bemerkungen zur Frage Charismen in der Kirche," in *Zeit Jesu* (Freiburg-Vienna, 1970), pp. 258–72, here p. 269.

29. 2Cel 148. A careful criticism contains the following episodes: after preaching to the people, according to LP 60, he often met alone with the priests, "so that the lay people did not hear him," and he admonished them about the care of souls and

the care of the sacred elements; he does not want papal writs with privileges (Testament); he behaves in a totally different way before the Sultan, in contrast to the violent strategy of the Christians. According to 2Cel 73, invited by Cardinal Hugolino, and faced with a well-set table, he gets up and goes out to beg alms, and only afterwards does he sit down at table, sharing the alms with the guests, saying: "I prefer a poor table, provisioned by alms, than such a full table, where the number of plates are countless."

30. Cf. R. Zerfas, *Der Streit um die Laienprendigt: Eine pastoral geschichtliche Untersuchung zum Verstandnis des Predigtamtes und su seiner Entwicklung im 12. und 13. Jahr hundert* (Freiburg, 1974); Francis is accused of "usurping the office of preaching"; Esteban de Borbon in *Escritos y biografias de san Francisco* (BAC, 1978), p. 973; the first brothers who went to Germany and France in 1217 were accused of being Albigensians and "heretics from Lombardy" (*Chronicle of Jordan de Giano* 4–5; TC 16).

31. E. Hoornaert, "Origem da 'vida religiosa' no Cristianismo," in *Perspectiva Teologica* 3 (1971), pp. 223–33.

32. For the visit of the Pope to the "favela" of Vidigal, in Rio de Janeiro, in July of 1980, a little chapel was built, and there was a survey of the people for the selection of a patron of the chapel. Curiously, Saint Francis had the majority of the votes, more than Christ and Mary.

33. LM 11, 1.

34. Ibid.

35. A. Schmucki, "Ignorans et idiota: Das Ausmass der Schulischen Bildung des hl. Franziskus von Assisi," in *Studia historico-eclesiastica: Festgabe an Prof. G. Spatling* (Rome, 1977), pp. 282–309. According to this researcher, Francis studied, when nine or ten years of age, in the Schola Minor, next to the church of St. George, in 1190–1191. With the aid of the psalter he learned to read and write, a bit of arithmetic, some liturgical songs and the basics of Christian life and doctrine. He did not pass elementary Latin and had to struggle to speak and write in Latin. He spoke and wrote with many errors; he also learned a little French. He was not a cultured man, and he fed his basic culture with the Holy Scriptures. The "ignorans et idiota" were scorned. Francis came to count himself among them.

36. 1R 17.

37. E. Peterson, "Der Monotheismus als politisches Problem," in *Theologische Traktate* (Munich, 1951).

38. LetF 56.

39. 1R 6.

40. Ibid., 5.

41. Adm 26; 1Cel 62; 2Cel 201.

42. Lm 15,5; 2Cel 216.

43. Test 14.

44. Cf. G. Volpe, *Movimenti religiosi e sette ereticali* (Florence, 1977), pp. 81–87; H. Grundmann, *Religiöse Bewegungen*, pp. 50–69; B. M. Bolton, "Tradition and Temerity: Papal Attitudes toward Deviants 1159–1216," in *Schism, Heresy and Religious Protest*, ed. O. Baker, (Cambridge, 1972), pp. 79–92.

45. *El proyecto evangelico de Francisco de Asis* (Madrid, 1978), p. 32.

46. 2Cel 10; LM 2,1.

47. 2Cel 17; LM 3,10; TC 12.

48. LetF 87; LetO 47; SalVir 17.

49. LetF 87.

50. 1R 24.

51. LetCle 14.

52. LetO 47.

53. LetF 1; LetAnth 1.

54. A. van Corstanje, *Gottes Bund mit den Armen* (Werl/West, 1964); C. Esser, *Das*

Testament des heiligen Franziskus von Assisi (Munster, 1949); A. Rotstetter, *Die Funktion der franziskanischen Bewegung*, pp. 98–104.

55. 2R, Prologue.
56. 2Cel 24.
57. 1R 19–21.
58. O. Schmucki, "Franziskus von Assisi erfahrt Kirche," p. 13.
59. LP 67; MP 26.
60. 2Cel 148.
61. See Rotzetter, *Die Funktion*, pp. 177–82, 249.
62. 1R 17.
63. Ibid. 7.
64. 2Cel 146; C. Esser, "Sancta Mater," pp. 168–79.
65. The Letter to All Clerics is wholly dedicated to this theme.
66. 1Cel 84.
67. 2Cel 192.
68. LP 62; 65.
69. 2R 6;1R 9.
70. Adm 7; 17.
71. LetF.
72. 2Cel 164.
73. 1Cel 52.
74. Ibid., 84–87.
75. Cf. G. Casagrande, "Una devozione moderna: la via crucis," in *Francescanessimo e società cittadina: l'esempio di Peruggia* (Perugia, 1979), pp. 265–88; the initiator was the Dominican Ricoldo de Monte Croce in 1294; later the Franciscan spread this devotion, beginning in Spain.
76. Cf. E. Delaruelle, "Saint François d'Assise et la piete populaire," in *San Francesco nella ricerca storica degli ultimi ottanta anni*, pp. 125–55; H. Hefele, *Die Bettelorden und das religiose Volksleben Oben-und-Mittel-Italiens im XIII. Jahrundert* (Leipzig-Berlin, 1910); A. Rotzetter, "Franz von Assisi zwischen Basis aund Hierarchie der Kirche," in Katholische Akademie Augsburg (Akademie Protokolle), *Franz von Assisi—ein Heiliger für unsere Zeit?* (Augsburg, 1976), pp. 28–57.
77. 1Cel 217; LM 15,5; see C. Esser, "Missarum solemnia," in *Temas espirituales*, pp. 227–79.
78. 2Cel 217.
79. See G. Wendelborn, *Franziskus von Assisi* (Vienna-Cologne-Graz, 1979), pp. 247–50; C. Esser, *La Orden Franciscana: Origenes e Ideales* (Aranzazu, 1976), pp. 72–79.
80. Testimonies compiled by C. Esser, *La Orden Franciscana*, p. 72.
81. The text is found in *Cronistas Franciscanos primitivos y otros documentos franciscanos del siglo XIII* (Santiago, Chile, 1981), p. 234.
82. See *São Francisco de Assis* (sources), p. 1028.
83. L. Boff, *El Rostro materno de Dios.*
84. J. Brady, *San Francesco, uomo dello Spirito* (Vicenza, 1978).
85. M. Ciccarelli, *I capisaldi della spiritualità francescana* (Milan, 1955), pp. 54–60, where the Holy Spirit is seen as the primary source of Franciscan spirituality.
86. See the principal texts with commentary in C. Esser, *Os Escritos de Sao Francisco de Assis* (Petropolis, 1979), pp. 228–33.
87. 2Cel 193.
88. Adm 9.
89. Especially the Praise of the Virtues, finale.
90. 1R 9; cf. O. Schmucki, "Franziskus von Assisi erfahrt Kirche," pp. 14–16, 21–23; C. Esser, *La Orden Franciscana*, pp. 195–201.
91. Test 31–34.
92. 1R 3.

93. See the beautiful reflections of A. Gemelli, *San Francesco d'Assisi e la sua "gente poverella"* (Milan, 1964), pp. 82–83.
94. Test 9–11.
95. Ibid.

Chapter 5—Integration of the Negative

1. The word is Greek in origin—*agōn*—and means struggle.
2. Phrase used by the well-known exegete E.-B. Allo in terms of Saint Paul in relation to Christ, and applied to Saint Francis by Y. Congar, "Saint François d'Assise ou l'Absolu de l'Evangile," in *Les voies du Dieu vivant* (Paris, 1962), pp. 247–64.
3. See the pertinent reflections of Rollo May upon love and the demonic in his book *Eros e Repressão* (Petropolis, 1972), pp. 136–97 [*Love and Will*].
4. Ibid., p. 166. In this context May cites the famous phrase of Rilke: "If my demons abandoned me, I fear that my angels would also leave me."
5. Cf. the suggestive work of E. Neumann, *Tiefenpsychologie und neue Ethik* (Zurich, 1968).
6. L. Boff, "Elementos de uma teología da crise," in *Credo para Amanhã*, III (Petropolis, 1972), pp. 169–98.
7. Words of Greek origin: *syn-ballein* means to join, unite, put together; *dia-ballein*, its antonym, that is, to take apart, to destroy.
8. See the study by Cajetan Esser with reference to the principal texts on the subject: "La enseñanza de san Francisco sobre la 'negación de sí,'" in *Temas espirituales*, pp. 45–72.
9. Fior, 9.
10. Ibid., 13.
11. 2Cel 123; Fior 10.
12. This narcissism shows itself, according to Celano, in the early childhood of Francis, when he says, for example: "Why do you think I am happy? I have the feeling that one day I will be venerated as a saint" (2Cel 4).
13. Lm. 8.
14. 2Cel 145.
15. MP 45.
16. Ibid.
17. LM 9, 1.
18. See the reflections of K. Beyschlag on mercy in Saint Francis, in *Die Bergpredigt und Franz von Assisi* (Gütersloch, 1955), pp. 189–200.
19. LetMin 5–11.
20. MP 46.
21. Ibid., 71; LP 76.
22. Rollo May, *Eros e Repressão*, p. 149.
23. A wider form, with additions of great theological content, is offered in *Fior* 8, whose redaction is placed between 1327 and 1340; see the parallels in other religious and spiritual planes: J. Sudbrack, "Die volkommene Freude: Aus den Legenden und Gotam Buddho und Franz von Assisi," in *Geist und Leben* 45 (1972), pp. 213–18; J. Lang, "Die volkommene Freude: Ein religiongeschichtlicher Vergleich zwischen Franziskus und den Chassidim," in *Franziskanische Studien* 58 (1976), pp. 47–54.
24. Fior 8.
25. Ibid.
26. LP 21; MP 99; 1Cel 115.
27. LP 114.
28. MP 11.
29. Ibid.

30. 1Cel 103; 2Cel 157.
31. LP 111; MP 1; LM 4, 1. Angel Clareno states that when the new text of the Rule was ready, "it was furtively stolen from Brother Leo, to whom the blessed Francis had sent it to keep, and they hid it, thinking that in this way they would deter the will of the saint to present it to the Holy Pontiff for his approval" (*Historia septem tribulationum*, ed. A. Ghinato [Rome, 1959], p. 59.; *Expositio Regulae*, ed. L. Oliger [Quaracchi, 1912], p. 9).
32. LP 113.
33. Ibid.
34. 2Cel 156.
35. MP 64; LP 83; 2Cel 145; LM 6, 3.
36. MP 41; 2Cel 188.
37. LP 76; MP 71.
38. 2Cel 158; LP 86; MP 81.
39. *Chronicle of Jordan de Giano*, 11–14.
40. 2Cel 81; MP 99; LP 21.
41. LP 77; MP 11.
42. Especially D. Flood, *Die Regula non bullata der Minderbruder* (Werl/West, 1967); L. Cautt, *Die älteste franziskanische Lebensform* (Graz, 1955); A. Rotzetter, "Der franziscanische Mensch zwischen Autorität und Freiheit," in *Franziskanische Studien* 59 (1977), pp. 97–124; L. Iriarte de Aspurz, "Lo que san Francisco hubiera querido decir en la Regla," in *Estudios franciscanos* 77 (1976), pp. 375–91.
43. See what is said in the *Legend of Perugia* 69: "The ministers knew very well that, according to the Rule, the brothers were bound to observe the holy gospel. Yet they had the passage in the rule that reads 'Take nothing for your journey' suppressed, since they thought they were not obliged to observe the perfection of the holy gospel. That is why blessed Francis, warned by the Holy Spirit of this mutilation, cried out in the presence of a few brothers: 'Do the ministers think they are making light of God and of me? Well, so that all the brothers may know and be forewarned that they are bound to observe the perfection of the Gospel, I wish it to be written in the beginning and at the end of the rule: the brothers are bound to observe the holy gospel of our Lord Jesus Christ.'"
44. 2Cel 193.
45. See the proper reflections of A. Ratzetter in the study cited above: "Der franziskanische Mensch," pp. 99, 118.
46. D. Vasse, *Le temps du désir* (Paris, 1969); A. Vergote, *Dette et désir* (Paris, 1978), pp. 164–84; C. Surian, *Elementi per una teologia del desiderio e la spiritualità di san Francesco d'Assisi* (Rome, 1973), pp. 66–69.
47. The most complete study on this topic is that of C. Surian cited in the previous note.
48. LP 17; MP 87; cf. O. Schmucki, "Gli ultimi due anni di san Francesco d'Assisi e il rinnovamento della nostra vita," in *Laurentianum* 17 (1976), pp. 208–50, esp. 242–50; S. Ciancarelli, *Francesco di Petro Bernardone malato e santo* (Florence, 1972), esp. 124–30.
49. 1Cel 107.
50. LM 14, 1.
51. LP 65; MP 122.
52. Ibid., 99; 121.
53. Ibid., 114.
54. Ibid., 99; MP 124; 1Cel 108.
55. 1Cel 109.
56. Ibid.
57. 2Cel 214; LM 14, 3.
58. Eloi Leclerc, *The Canticle of the Creatures* (Chicago, 1977).
59. 2Cel 214.

60. 2Cel 216.
61. Ibid.
62. *Rule of Saint Clare* 6; LP 109; MP 108.
63. LP 101; MP 112; 3Cel 37–39.
64. 2Cel 217; LP 117; MP 88; LM 14, 4.
65. 2Cel 217.
66. Ibid.
67. For a philosophical-theological theory of death, see L. Boff, *Hablemos de la otra vida* (Madrid); id., *A Resurreição de Cristo e a Nossa na Morte* (Petropolis, 1980).
68. LM 7, 2.
69. Sigmund Freud, *Vida e Agonía*, 3 (Rio de Janeiro, 1981), pp. 642–43.